KT-504-705

Edward Stourton is the author of five previous books. He is a newspaper columnist, writer and presenter of several high-profile current affairs programmes and documentaries for radio and television, and regularly presents BBC Radio Four programmes such as *The World at One*, *The World this Weekend*, *Sunday* and *Analysis*. He is a frequent contributor to the *Today* programme, where for ten years he was one of the main presenters.

www.**transworldbooks**.co.uk

04214453

Diary of a Dog-Walker:

Time spent following a lead

Edward Stourton

BLACK SWAN

TRANSWORLD PUBLISHERS
61–63 Uxbridge Road, London W5 5SA
A Random House Group Company
www.transworldbooks.co.uk

DIARY OF A DOG-WALKER
A BLACK SWAN BOOK: 9780552777278

First published in Great Britain
in 2011 by Doubleday
an imprint of Transworld Publishers
Black Swan edition published 2012

Addresses for Random House Group Ltd companies outside the UK
can be found at: www.randomhouse.co.uk
The Random House Group Ltd Reg. No. 954009

The Random House Group Limited supports The Forest Stewardship Council® (FSC®), the
leading international forest-certification organisation. Our books carrying the FSC label are
printed on FSC®-certified paper. FSC is the only forest-certification scheme supported by the
leading environmental organisations, including Greenpeace. Our paper procurement policy
can be found at www.randomhouse.co.uk/environment

Typeset in Berkeley Book by Falcon Oast Graphic Art Ltd.
Printed in the UK by CPI Group (UK) Ltd, Croydon, CR0 4YY.

6 8 10 9 7

MIX
Paper from
responsible sources
FSC   FSC® C016897
www.fsc.org

To Fiona, Eleanor and Rosy, the women in Kudu's life

Acknowledgements

In dark moments I have cringed at my own presumption in imagining that people would be interested in me and my dog, and I am grateful to those who have kept faith with a project that might easily have been dismissed as preposterous. Rhidian Wynn-Davies originally championed the column at the *Daily Telegraph*, Vivienne Schuster, my tireless agent, saw the potential for a book, and Susanna Wadeson, my editor at Transworld, showed me – very tactfully – how to shape the material into one.

My writing has often been improved by a loyal team of readers and editors at the kitchen table and in the *Telegraph* newsroom, and most of all I owe gratitude to those who have supplied the stories, the dog-walkers of Battersea and Clapham first among them. Anne Whiteside, who walks Kudu when I am away, deserves special mention for taking such wonderfully good care of him. David Nissan and Gwyneth Williams nurtured him during the first weeks of his life, so this book really could not have been written without them; when their litter was broken up they kept one of Kudu's sisters, Mielie, for themselves, and we heard with great sadness that she had died of pancreatitis at the tender age of three and a half.

I have quoted widely from the canon of dog literature, and would like to thank the following authors and estates for permission to use their works: *In Search of Fatima* © 2002, Ghada Karmi, Verso Books; *Spies of the Balkans* © 2010, Alan Furst, Weidenfeld & Nicolson, an imprint of The Orion Publishing Group, London; *Man Meets Dog* by Konrad Lorenz ©1983, Deutscher Taschenbuch Verlag GmbH & Co. KG, Munich, Germany; *Inside of a Dog* © 2009 by Alexandra Horowitz, Simon and Schuster; *Dogs and Their Ancestors* by Mrs Neville Lytton, printed with permission of The Earl of Lytton; *My Dog Tulip* by J. R. Ackerley © 1965, Methuen, London; *The Old Brown Dog* © 1985, Coral Lansbury, The University of Wisconsin Press.

1

Letting a Dog Into Your Life

Diary of a Dog-Walker
Daily Telegraph, *Saturday, 30 May 2009*

ONE OF THE Dog's admirable qualities is an instinct for friends with elegant owners, and it is a glamorous gaggle that gathers around the bandstand on this fine May morning. We are in Battersea Park, across the river from Chelsea, and one or two of the hacking jackets on display are cut with just a little more dash than is strictly necessary for dog-walking.

They are all there – the sniffers and trotters, the sprinters and plodders, the yappers and slobberers, the shaggy and the *soigné*. While they do their doggy thing about our feet, we, their masters and mistresses (or perhaps their servants?), do ours. We talk. Here, I have discussed everything from high politics in the Middle East to the low points of divorce, from children and jobs through plays, books and exhibitions to holiday homes, the credit crunch, and – of course – canine triumphs and tragedies. This easy-going social intercourse is the great revelation of dog-owning in middle age. If you are accompanied by a dog you can talk to anyone, and anyone can talk to you – about anything.

To get there, you need the capacity for benign amnesia that allows mothers to repeat the pain of childbirth and authors to submit themselves to the racking anxieties of a new book. I once shared my life with a rumbustious Spabrador (a Spaniel/Labrador cross) but even her most searing indiscretions have now been rose-tinted into jolly anecdotes. When she was a puppy my daughter trained her to use a sheet of newspaper as her lavatory: one Sunday morning she jumped on to the bed as I was reading the *Sunday Telegraph* and, before you could say 'Pavlov', there it was, hot and steaming in the middle of a piece of finely crafted prose from Sir Peregrine Worsthorne (no offence, I am sure, intended).

You also need a post-modernist ability to hold two completely contradictory views simultaneously in your mind. We who make our regular pilgrimage to Battersea Park know that a dog is just a dog (whatever the park's splendid Buddhist Temple may hint to the contrary), that it will never write a great book or win a Nobel Prize. We know that evolution has taught it the charm that compels our attention to its wants and needs. And yet we allow ourselves to speak and think of dogs as friends, individuals with a full claim on our affections.

The reward is that dog-walking becomes like reading a novel, or watching a play: disbelief is suspended and, for an hour or so, we are given licence to escape ordinary life. Fantasy flourishes, and really quite trivial moments in dog life become a source of wonder to be repeated, discussed, laughed about and even worried over with its human family.

The novel the Dog and I enjoy in Battersea is at the Jane Austen end of the market. He can do a noble profile that would put Mr Darcy to shame. One of his admirers, while skiing in St Moritz, bought him a collar studded with golden cows; it gives him the slightly foppish air of the Alexander Pope dog whose collar carried the legend

'I am his Highness' Dog at Kew;
Pray tell me sir, whose dog are you?'

And I was once approached in the park with an unsolicited proposal of marriage, conditional, of course, on a full inspection of his pedigree (the lady in question, with a home off the King's Road and a weekend shooting habit, could not have been a more suitable bride, but sadly the pedigrees revealed that his father was her grandfather).

Here, at home in his local park, he has a south-London life that is more *Trainspotting* than *Pride and Prejudice*. Not many of his smart Chelsea friends have looked up from their snuffling to see a heroin addict lowering his trousers in search of a vein that still works. There is a Stockwell swagger to the Dog's style, fancy collar notwithstanding.

His name is Kudu. In the next of these columns I shall introduce him more fully – and explain where he may take us. Then we shall follow his nose.

I was over fifty and a hardened hack, but I was as nervous as hell when I sent in that first column.

I sat down to write it and stared at the cursor at the top of an empty screen. It brought on a terrible failure of nerve. The nice thing about mainstream news journalism is that you do not generally have to work too hard to persuade the audience to engage; if you are reporting a war or a superpower summit, or interviewing a president or a prime minister (I've done six of the last eight British ones, which makes me feel dreadfully old), it is fairly self-evident why the story matters. Could I really persuade people that my daily doings with the dog were a 'must read' on a Saturday morning?

Because I have worked – mostly – as a broadcaster, I have spent all my professional life ruthlessly excluding any hint of personal opinion from my output; a column, of course, is an entirely personal piece of writing. And while scripting for broadcast means being direct, simple and, above all, linear (lesson number one: a viewer or listener cannot go back to the beginning of the story if they miss something in the way a newspaper reader might), the columnist's art lies in discursive sallies and a judicious seasoning of baroque stylistic curlicues.

So, what a relief it was when the paper thudded on to the mat that Saturday morning and the piece was really there. My wife pointed out unkindly that Kudu's head-shot was rather more flattering than mine, but it was still a milestone moment in my journalistic career.

The column was an accidental child of a rather miserable moment in my professional life. In December 2008 I learnt that I was losing my job as a presenter of Radio 4's *Today* programme. One of the unexpected consequences was the discovery that I was a popular figure with the readers of the *Daily Telegraph*. The newspaper ran a campaign on my behalf and a surprisingly (and very gratifyingly) large number of them wrote in to support it. When the dust had settled, a senior member of the paper's editorial team got in touch to ask whether I would be interested in writing for them on a regular basis.

I felt rather sheepish when I pitched the idea of making Kudu's life the focus for my contributions: it was about the time the paper was beginning its revelations about MPs' expenses, a story that has had a profound and lasting impact on the character of British politics. Dog-walking seemed a tad trivial by comparison. But, to my great delight, the bigwigs gave the proposal a thumbs-up.

Laurence Sterne's character Tristram Shandy attributes his obsession with the subject of Time to the conversation that took place between his parents at the moment of his conception: '*Pray, my dear,* quoth my mother,' he writes in his *Life and Opinions*, '*have you not forgot to wind up the clock? – Good G-!* cried my father, making an exclamation, but taking care to moderate his voice at the same time – *Did ever woman, since the creation of the world, interrupt a man with such a silly question?*' Kudu's journalistic future was perhaps sealed in the same way because he was conceived – as a concept, rather than literally – in the course of a longish liquid lunch.

The great journalistic tradition of lunchtime boozing on a heroic scale is almost dead now. In 1979, when I joined ITN as a graduate trainee, the entire staff would abandon the building for the pubs and restaurants of Fitzrovia and Soho. The general reporters only really had to work if they were assigned a story, so they would simply set up camp in a restaurant called the Montebello in Great Portland Street, merrily pouring red wine down their throats until the news desk called on the restaurant phone (no mobiles in those days, of course). If you had a contact to entertain it was Bertorelli's, L'Escargot or the Gay Hussar, and the company paid.

Nowadays we are all far too busy – and, anyway, the culture will not allow it; *Private Eye*'s perennial caricature

Lunchtime O'Booze should really be renamed Lunchtime No Booze. Journalists are a good deal healthier as a result, and I, for one, do not have anything like the stamina I had then – much more than a glass at lunch and I need a power nap (actually more of a siesta) to recover. But I regret the passing of the institution. Contacts sometimes told you things over lunch – real stories that no one else knew about. And it was, above all, a chance to discuss ideas, swap gossip and generally ruminate on the World in a relaxed and expansive way. It made journalism – dare I say it? – fun. I was lucky enough to be part of the wonderfully inventive team that got *Channel 4 News* off the ground, and quite a lot of the creative juices that made the programme the institution it is today were released by Charlotte Street pasta and Chianti.

So, on those rare occasions when the chance of a good old-fashioned journalistic lunch pops up, I'm afraid I leap at it. In the aftermath of 11 September 2001 I made several radio series about the impact of that terrible day. The formula was simple: persuade as many as possible of the key political and diplomatic players to talk to us, ask them to tell their stories, and then weave the different accounts together. It worked better than we could have hoped. Sometimes, if we were lucky, we managed to put together both sides of a telephone conversation between senior politicians from different capitals, and the narrative could be compelling. But it was hard pounding, and at the end of each of these epic efforts the exhausted producer, editor and I would go out to lunch together to celebrate.

It was in the course of one of these convivial, very mildly boozy (wimpishly so, by the standards of the 1970s and early 1980s) lunches that our editor mentioned her English Springer Spaniel bitch was pregnant. There was a waiting list for the puppies, but there might – who knew? It depended on the size of the litter – still be a couple that needed homes . . .

It was one of those moments when a constellation of factors comes propitiously together. I was about to begin a new book, so I knew that for the next six months or so I would be avoiding too many foreign trips. And having been a dog-owner when I wrote my first book, I remembered what useful aids to creativity they can be: when your head feels clogged with facts, a good stomp through greenery can be just what it needs to shake them into a shape that makes sense.

And my life on the *Today* programme seemed settled then. The *Today* working pattern means being in the office when everyone else is at home (I used to leave at three forty a.m. and get home just before ten) and being at home when everyone else is in the office – so the dog would not be left alone for long stretches. Finally (I kept quiet about this one) I rather fancied some male company: at the time, the other members of our household were my wife, my daughter, my stepdaughter and two cats (one male, but he had been neutered, so he didn't quite count); the mix needed gender balancing.

My daughter Eleanor, and Rosy, my stepdaughter, were, of course, enthusiastic allies in the dog project. Convincing my wife that we should have another animal – and a much more high-maintenance one than the cats – proved trickier, and I had to give a guarantee in blood that he would be my sole responsibility. She was thus persuaded into an exploratory family expedition to inspect the litter – 'No commitments, just to see if we like the idea.'

As she was leaving the office that afternoon one of her colleagues threw her a piece of worldly wisdom: 'If you've got to this stage,' he said, 'you won't be deciding whether, you'll be deciding which one.' She came very close to changing her mind.

In the end Kudu took matters into his own paws: as we peered into the squealing mass of warm flesh in the puppy box, he pushed through his brothers and sisters and tried to climb up Rosy's arm. That was it.

And for a while it all went swimmingly. There were, of course, a few teething problems. The cats peered into his box when he arrived and, with comedy H. M. Bateman-like expressions of indignation, headed over the garden wall. It was at least a week before they moved back in. I caught the new arrival trying to take a dump behind the sofa in the drawing room, but he looked guilty even as he was doing it, and a shout from me ensured it was a one-off. By and large the house-training process was achieved with remarkably little damage to the fixtures and fittings.

He was nervous on his first outings to the local park – there were some embarrassing moments when he squatted on the ground and refused to move – but he soon got the point, and within a few weeks he and I had settled into a rhythm: I would return from a *Today* shift, take him to Battersea Park or

Clapham Common for a head-clearing walk, and then the two of us would repair to the garden shed where I do my writing.

Kudu made a very early literary début. My book was about political correctness, and one of the problems that preoccupied me on those early walks was how far politics should dictate the language we use – whether, for example, a female chairman should be called a chair, a chairperson or, as the *New York Times* once wittily suggested, a chairperdaughter. My answer flowed from the idea that naming a person or a thing is a mechanism for asserting power – the way Adam is given the power to name the animals in the Book of Genesis being the earliest example.

To illustrate the power of naming, I related the intense family battle there had been about Kudu's name. It was the early days of the Facebook phenomenon, so everyone, including members of the family who were not living with us, could join in. In my book I described 'a ferocious tit-for-tat of proposal and counter-proposal between my stepdaughter and my daughter, names flashing back and forth like an exchange of machine-gun fire . . . My younger son, on his gap year somewhere in the Amazon rainforest, occasionally sent facetious suggestions via the Internet. "I met a lovely Brazilian girl who called herself Madame FruFru – any chance of me pitching that to the board?" and simply "Meatflaps" were examples of the sort of unhelpful ideas we found waiting in our Facebook inboxes. The elder son was superior ("Psmith with a silent P?"), and more upmarket ideas floated in from his girlfriend ("Truman" and "Benedict" among them) . . .' All this,

I argued, had much more to do with power-relationships within the family than it did with the dog.

I concluded that in principle people should be allowed to choose the way they would like to be described. If someone who is visually impaired would rather be referred to as 'partially sighted', why not respect that? The idea that we should – as a default position at least – take people at the estimation they place on themselves seems civilized to me, and I called it the Kudu Principle because the dog helped me formulate it.

Kudu helped me in one other significant way during those early months of his life. I am, by nature, a gregarious fellow, and writing a book is a solitary business. The *Today* team are a jolly bunch, but because the presenter's job means an office life of a couple of hours' intense preparation followed by three hours of live broadcasting it is a little like being a soldier who only joins his unit when they go into battle; there isn't much opportunity for gossip and idle chat. This is a sad fact to admit, but increasingly I found that my social life became focused around walking the dog.

He was such a pretty puppy that no one we met could resist smiling at him and talking to me. And very relaxing it was to chat to people with a common interest that had nothing whatever to do with the matters that generally preoccupied me during working hours.

By the time I began writing my dog columns my professional life had changed dramatically, but when I re-read these first pieces I am reminded of the carefree spirit of those early dog-walking days.

Commodore Coco Fluffy Paws
is no name for a dog
13 June 2009

The Dog's best Battersea friend is called Achilles. The name was inspired by a young boy's affectionate and rather good joke against his mother: endless fun, he thought, could be had from hearing her call, 'Achilles . . . heel!'

Being a Spaniel, Achilles doesn't really do heel. He can, however, lay claim (I suspect) to being the only dog in SW1 to have a Homeric Epithet. In *The Iliad*, the description 'fleet-footed' is almost always attached to the name of Achilles, and as the glorious streak of sprinting gold that bears the mythical warrior's name disappears in pursuit of some deliciously dead piece of London wildlife, the phrase suits him all too well.

Finding a name that fits your dog is hazardous – the madness that brought it into your life can tempt you into exuberance. Our neighbours have just negotiated the siren temptations of 'Duke Pompom of Stockwell', 'Commodore Coco Fluffy Paws', and Tinchy (after Tinchy Strider, a rapper, since you ask), but settled on the perfectly sensible and appropriate 'Teddy' for their Poodle.

Our own Dog was named in honour of his ancestral heritage: his mother's owners have a South

African background, and their animals are named in Zulu and Afrikaans. Our search for something suitable turned up one name I rather regret: Iska means 'the wind' in the West African language Hausa. It is melodious, but that final *a* gives it a feminine feel, and the Dog is very blokeish – so I offer it to any reader seeking a name for a fleet-footed bitch.

We chose Kudu for our Springer Spaniel because the beast that bears that name is large and springs – and, with Dog-Vanity-by-Proxy (or DVP, a surprisingly common psychological condition), because the nineteenth-century hunter Frederick Selous described the kudu as 'perhaps the handsomest antelope in the world'. Further research reveals that male kudus are known for the way they 'avoid violent situations and prefer to side-step danger rather than create it'.

The Dog shows remarkable emotional intelligence in this regard. There is some rough trade about on Clapham Common, and his method of dealing with aggression is straight out of the manual we BBC types learn when we are sent on courses about operating in Hostile Environments.

If you are kidnapped, we are told, try not to draw attention to yourself, but at the same time be friendly, and on no account be so grovelling and submissive that the kidnappers feel they can treat you as less than human: that makes you the most likely candidate in a kidnap group to be killed.

Kudu's response to one of those growling broad-shouldered types that sometimes swagger up with evil intent on the common is to stand very still with a wagging tail. Everything offers friendship, but there is something of substance about the way he holds himself. He never barks – but very, very occasionally, and only if the back-end sniffing turns nasty, he can do a decent throat-gurgle.

He has formed a pact with the household cats. They sometimes ask for food and then quite deliberately leave the bowl for him – he rewards them (sorry about this) with a bottom-lick. ('Just like the office, really,' remarked one of my friends.)

The shrubberies of Battersea Park have, during the damp dog-walking days of the crisis created by the unfolding revelations about MPs' expenses, been haunted by MPs' spouses, whose spending habits have featured in the newspapers. When the first of these columns appeared, I sent a text message to an MP friend who suffers badly from DVP; his constituents would be quite shocked by the depth of his passion for Magda, his fine-boned Welsh Springer.

My message read, **Hope you have seen handsomest dog in Britain on front page of Daily Telegraph.** He was in Singapore at the time, and a nervous question came back: **Why is Magda on front of D Tel? Have they worked out that I employ her as my diary secretary?**

Nearly two and a half thousand years ago the prolific Greek writer Xenophon – who seems to have had views on just about everything – wrote a treatise on how puppies should be trained for hunting, and it includes a passage of instruction on naming them. It could have been written yesterday. He says the names should be short so the dogs can be easily called, and the list he offers suggests that the Ancient Greeks liked to project human qualities on to their pets in just the way that we do. Here are some of my favourites:

Thymus, meaning 'courage'
Porpax, meaning 'shield hasp' – a little anachronistic, but the pun is fun
Psyche, meaning 'spirit'; a beautiful word, although I suppose it could lead to misunderstanding today
Phylax, meaning 'keeper'; good for a guard dog
Xiphon, meaning 'darter'; perfect for a Whippet
Phonax, meaning 'barker'
Phlegon, meaning 'fiery'; pretentious to modern ears, perhaps, but worth the social risk for a really noble beast – say, a Mastiff?
Alce, meaning 'strength'
Chara, meaning 'gladness'

Augo, meaning 'bright eyes'

Bia, meaning 'force' – but, like the Hausa word 'Iska', tricky for a male dog because it sounds feminine

Oenas, meaning 'reveller'

Actis, meaning 'ray' (as in sunlight)

Horme, meaning 'eager' – just right for a dog like Kudu, although of course people would make it 'horny', and just occasionally he is that too

I did not discover this list until long after we had named Kudu, and I am almost tempted to get another dog simply for the pleasure of choosing one of these names. In almost every case the original Greek word is so much sweeter on the ear than its modern English equivalent.

The heat is on and it's time to escape old haunts
27 June 2009

The lake at Battersea has turned whiffy in the heat – one of the Chelsea ladies declared it 'could do with a jolly good hoover'. The joggers are there in droves, sweating about the place in a purposeful way quite at odds with the agreeable aimlessness of the damp-weather dog-walking crowd.

A book I have been recommended opens with a reference to the park's 'popular cottaging areas adjacent to the public toilets and the athletics track'

– it is almost a throwaway line, as if everyone knows, but it is news to me and, I am sure, to the Dog.

Familiar haunts suddenly feel alien. It is time to escape.

Dogs need to believe that their owners behave logically – just as soldiers must, to stay sane and brave, believe in the wisdom of their generals, and priests in the compassion of their gods. The Dog has formed the view – on the sound evidentiary basis of experience – that green spaces are designed for his pleasure. As we drove past Hyde Park without stopping, his usually phlegmatic disposition gave way to indignation, moving up through the gears to squealing hysteria by the time we hit the A1.

Kudu has become a minor celebrity: the *Stockwell News* gave him a headline after my disobliging comments about our local park. But his host at our destination, a venerable Border Collie, was the real thing. Bertie's home is rented out to filmmakers, and he has had several pad-on parts. Kudu treated him with due deference.

Bertie's coup was being stroked by Geraldine James while the 'Bitty' scene in *Little Britain* was being recorded. Readers unfamiliar with 'Bitty' should think carefully before they look for it on YouTube. I was shown it just before a *Today* discussion about breast-feeding, and it is most unsettling. Small wonder a look of existential angst occasionally clouds

Bertie's thoughtful eyes: which of us, after a lifetime of faithful family service and dreams of sheep, could assimilate the sight of a chap manipulating a milk-squirting pump behind the sofa?

Bertie's owner – a distinguished lawyer, who therefore has firm views on everything – believes that a dog's intelligence can be judged by the words it knows. Bertie, he claims, understands all the variations of 'ride': whether it is 'shall we go for a ride?' or 'Let's go riding now', the dog is off to the tack room. Kudu has a similar learnt response to the Saturday-morning moment when my wife puts her walking jeans on: he becomes so frenzied as denim covers leg that she now delays dressing until the last minute, adding a scandalously exciting dimension of wifely semi-nudity to weekend pleasures.

We set off, with me on foot and Bertie's owner on his horse, and were soon in one of those secret stretches of English countryside that fold in on themselves to keep their wildness private. We were less than twenty miles from London – we passed Stratton's Folly, a tower built by an eighteenth-century merchant so that he could admire his ships on the Thames – but this was still the Hertfordshire that Beatrix Potter loved when she visited her grandmother at Essendon (we could hear its parish bells across the fields).

Kudu's most elegant manoeuvre is the Scentguided High-speed Handbrake Turn: when the nose hits something sniffable, it locks on, like a laser to a Tornado, and, whatever his speed, the rest of him swings round it as he decelerates. Watching him work the hedgerows with focused enthusiasm was just the tonic I needed.

The sniff-centric world-view can make him forget himself, and he has, I fear, been known to lift a leg on a fellow dog-walker's boots. I once watched impotently as, running ahead, his nose locked on to the shoes of Battersea's most celebrated walker, Lady Thatcher.

But there is a fine political instinct in that solid-chocolate head: at the *moment critique* the leg uncocked, and she gave him a gracious smile.

The day Jim Naughtie and I broke all the rules
11 July 2009

A cardinal rule of broadcasting is never to run: if you arrive breathless in the studio it is impossible to recover. Another is that two presenters should never talk together: the listeners hate it. And if you raise your voice – there are exceptions to this – you have probably lost control.

Dog-walking is different. My *Today* colleague

James Naughtie and I took to Richmond Park on the hottest afternoon of the heatwave. The park is the capital's giant lung (far and away London's largest open space), and you breathe more easily within its gates. Even after days of pitiless sun those majestic aspects – with their oaks and deer – looked temptingly lush.

The Spaniels took off. Jim's Tess – a ten-year-old Cocker of usually dignified demeanour – spotted a picnic, and the snout was among the sandwiches. My Kudu sprinted to an oak to defecate – a yard from an elderly lady enjoying her book in the shade. The crimes, satisfyingly symmetrical in a curious way, were simultaneous, and Jim and I broke all those broadcasting rules at once as we restored decorum.

Jim made his confession: in South Africa recently he ate a steak from the Kudu antelope. Mrs Naughtie, he reported, had shown greater scruple, and declined the dish out of respect for the Dog. I salute her sensitivity.

To the dogs, Richmond offered smells of real country. To me this royal park smells of power; the ghosts of Tudors and Stuarts hunt here, and from Henry's Mound you can look down on Westminster. We fell to talking about dogs and politics.

Richard Nixon hated the fact that one of his most famous speeches became identified with the family Spaniel. Running for the vice-presidency in 1952, he faced accusations of financial impropriety. He responded with a television address that saved his place on the Republican ticket.

After a robust defence of his family's 'modest' lifestyle, he owned up to one gift from a political well-wisher. 'You know what it was?' he asked. 'It was a little Cocker Spaniel dog in a crate . . . Black-and-white spotted. And our little girl – Tricia, the six-year-old – named it Checkers. And, you know, the kids, like all kids, love the dog and I just want to say this right now that, regardless of what they say about it, we're gonna keep it.'

That became known as 'the Checkers Speech'. Nixon complained it was 'as though the mention of my dog was the only thing that saved my political career'. Bad news for Spaniel lovers like me: if it had not been for Checkers, there might never have been a Watergate.

Jim loves American politics; I am fascinated by the French version. I offered an example of the superiority of French culture: the most perceptive biography of the late President François Mitterrand is *Le Gros Secret*, attributed to his Labrador Baltique.

Baltique listened as her master quizzed Helmut Kohl about a sauerkraut recipe that might be rich enough to send Margaret Thatcher to sleep at an EU summit (my memory is that it was usually Mitterrand who succumbed to snoozing at these events, but there we go). We learn that Mitterrand bugged Baltique's toys and sent her to drop them in the offices of those he suspected of disloyalty. And hours of presidential time were spent in training her to pee on Edouard Balladur's Savile Row trousers.

Le Gros Secret now costs more than it did when I bought it new in 1995; I suspect its appeal lies beyond the taste of oddballs like me, who are nerdy about modern French politics. Baltique's desolation as she watches her master decay and die makes her drama, not the president's, the real story. It is a book about the way we hope dogs feel about us.

On my return from a recent trip abroad, Kudu greeted me with his muzzle buried between his paws, quivering as if emotion had overcome him. Small wonder we anthropomorphize.

A pooch knows who's master and commander
25 July 2009

'I think your dog is lovely,' said my neighbour, at a Devon dinner party. 'Your wife seems very nice too.'

Kudu had distinguished himself with good behaviour, and was looking magnificent stretched luxuriously on a Turkey rug; it took a beat before I realized I was being teased. Then it was like the moment I opened the fourth cigarette packet in a single day – it was during the siege of Sarajevo, so things were stressful – and understood that I had to get a grip on my addiction: time to take stock of the Dog Habit.

My Church is stern about the proper relationship between humans and animals. 'By a most just ordinance of the Creator,' wrote St Augustine, 'both their life and their death are subject to our own use.' Thomas Aquinas proposed the concept of a hierarchy of creation, in which humans sit above animals and are therefore entitled to use them as they see fit.

This sort of stuff has given Catholicism a reputation for heartless speciesism, but the sound common sense behind it was brought home to me the morning after my sobering Devon dinner.

Walking in the Blackdown Hills, our host lost his way as we tried to cut back towards the village of Kentisbeare. 'Better put the dogs on a lead,' he suggested, as we approached a farmyard. It was a smart move. The farmer yelled as only an angry farmer can, berating us for straying from the footpath. We listened patiently, apologized unreservedly, and then pointed out, by way of mitigation, that the dogs were under control. Angry farmer became calmer, conceded the point and, still grumbling a bit, allowed us to proceed on our way.

The dogs did not want to be put on leads at that point: it was an intoxicatingly fresh morning, and

Kudu strained at his throughout the exchange. We were using them entirely for our own end: the negotiation of a peaceful passage.

Dogs are incredibly valuable tools in this regard. Walking with a dog always improves the quality of my interaction with other people, and I feel confident about my right to 'use' Kudu as a social asset in this way. When a small child wants to stroke him I make the Dog sit for a while; valuable dog time is lost, but the sum of human happiness is increased. Kudu does not especially enjoy this, but he accepts it.

But the Thomist approach to dog-walking is unfashionable. I chaired a Radio 4 lecture by Professor Peter Singer, the intellectual father of the Animal Rights Movement, and it was an unnerving experience: he is a charming and persuasive man, who can lead you into accepting monstrous propositions.

Singer believes that sentience, not reason, is the key to rights; to discriminate against a dog – which can feel pleasure and pain – is like discriminating because of skin colour. He argues that a disabled human may be less intelligent than an animal, and that infanticide is not the same as murder because a newborn lacks consciousness. The logic is that it may be more reasonable to 'put down' a sick child than a dog.

My answer is the story of Elinor Goodman's Pointers.

The distinguished political commentator – a Battersea Park regular – described the death of her elder dog, Ash. A blanket was laid out on the lawn, and Ash was given a piece of chicken while the vet went about his business. All this was watched by the younger Beagle, Florrie, from the french windows.

Once the body had been taken away, Florrie bounded out and began scrabbling in the death-blanket. Elinor assumed this was a doggy farewell to a friend and companion. But Florrie was simply looking for the chicken.

I like to think that my wife would react differently to my own demise. In the end a dog – even the Dog – is just a dog. And very happy like that they are.

2

An Imprudent Affection

'THUS IT WAS Melissa who figured it out, sensed it, before he did. Zannis must have dozed because, just after dawn, she growled, a subdued, speculative sort of growl – *what's this?* And Zannis woke up.

'Melissa? What goes on?'

She stood at the window, *out there*, turned her head and stared at him as he unwound himself from the snarled bedding. What had caught her attention, he realized, were voices, coming from below, on Santaroza Lane. Agitated, fearful voices. Somebody across the street had a window open and the radio on. It wasn't music – Zannis couldn't make out the words but he could hear the tone of voice, pitched low and grim.'

The spy-writer Alan Furst has the hero's dog announce the invasion of Greece by the Italians in 1940, a pivotal moment in his book *Spies of the Balkans*. I am a huge Furst fan: his prose has the stark clarity of a black-and-white photo (he is also clearly a dog-lover) and the way he uses Melissa here is characteristic of the subtlety that allows him to pack so much into his relatively short thrillers.

We meet her early in the book: she is a mountain dog, 'a big girl, eighty pounds, with a thick soft black-and-white coat and a smooth face, long muzzle and beautiful eyes', with strongly developed guard-dog instincts. Her daily routine goes like this: 'Queen of the street, she started her morning by walking him [Zannis, the hero] a few blocks towards the office, to a point where, instinct told her, he was no longer in danger of being attacked by wolves. Next she returned home to protect the local kids on their way to school, then accompanied the postman on his rounds. That done, she would guard the chicken coop in a neighbour's courtyard, head resting on massive paws.'

Zannis takes her to dinner with his mother once a week, and she emerges as a central figure in the easy-going pre-war life he enjoys as a policeman in the Greek port of Salonika. So, by giving her centre stage at the moment of high drama when the war arrives at Zannis's front door, Furst gently reminds us of everything his hero has to lose.

The Palestinian writer Ghada Karmi pulls off the same trick in her memoir *In Search of Fatima*. Her dog Rex is held up as a kind of symbol of the life she enjoyed as the child of a professional Palestinian family in the Jerusalem of the mid-1940s, when the British ruled Palestine under a UN mandate. Believing firmly in British might and British good faith, the family are slow to accept the growing evidence that a Jewish state is inevitable. Living happily and comfortably, they are reluctant to believe that their lives could be disrupted by violence and war. When they are finally forced to accept reality, by the war of 1948, it is almost too late:

> 'Ghada! Come on, come on, please!' Rex inside the iron garden gate, she outside. The house with its empty veranda shuttered and closed, secretive and already mysterious, as if they had never lived there and it had never been their home. The fruit trees in the garden stark against the morning sky.
>
> Every nerve and fibre of her being raged against her fate, the *cruelty* of leaving that she was powerless to avert. She put her palms up against the gate and Rex started barking and pushing at it, thinking she was coming in. Her mother dragged her away and pushed her into the back seat of the taxi on to Fatima's lap. The rest got in and Muhammad banged the car doors shut. She twisted round, kneeling to look out of the back window.
>
> Another explosion. The taxi, which had seen better days, revved loudly and started to move off. But through the back window, a terrible sight, which only she could see, Rex had somehow got out, was

standing in the middle of the road. He was still and silent, staring after their retreating car, his tail stiff, his ears pointing forward.

With utter clarity, the little girl saw in that moment that he knew what she knew, that they would never meet again.

The prose is every bit as spare and urgent as Alan Furst's, and this is, if anything, an even more poignant passage because it is a true story. Ghada Karmi's snapshot memory also brings home the blood-draining sense of impotence that accompanies moments of great disaster. The dog–human relationship is based on a deal: in return for all the love they lavish on us, we will look after them when the chips are down. But when the tide of history overwhelms us, we humans welsh on the deal. We never find out what happened to Rex, but he is often in our minds as we read the pages that follow.

Discovering that I was losing my job as a presenter of Radio 4's *Today* programme was not quite on a par with the Axis invasion of Greece or the Naqba, the Disaster, as Palestinians call the events described by Ghada Karmi, but it was a bit of a blow in the Stourton household. And, in retrospect, I am surprised by the amount of time I spent thinking about the dog in the emotional period that followed. Grim, big thoughts (of the 'I've passed my peak, from now it's all downhill to death' variety) jostled with much more trivial concerns about canine care: what would happen to Kudu, I wondered, if I had to get a proper job with normal hours? Who would walk him? What if I got a new job that did not pay well enough for me to afford a dog-walker?

Kudu's response was that very doggy worried look, eyebrows arched in an expression of distressed puzzlement. 'I don't know what the problem is,' he seemed to be saying, 'but I am most frightfully sorry about it, whatever it is . . . Now, can we put that to one side and go for a walk?'

Jerome K. Jerome – of *Three Men in a Boat* fame – has this very good description of the way pets respond to upset owners:

> When we bury our face in our hands and wish we had never been born, they don't sit up very straight, and observe that we have brought it all upon ourselves. They don't even hope it will be a warning to us.
>
> But they come up softly and shove their heads against us. If it is a dog, he looks up at you with his big true eyes, and says with them, 'Well, you've always got me, you know. We'll go through the world together, and always stand by each other, won't we?'
>
> He is very imprudent, a dog is. He never makes it his business to inquire whether you are in the right or in the wrong, never bothers as to whether you are going up or down on life's ladder, never asks whether you are rich or poor, silly or wise, a saint or a sinner. Come luck or misfortune, good repute or bad, honour or shame, he is going to stick with you, to

comfort you, guard you and give his life for you, if need be . . . You are his pal, that is enough for him.

It all rings very true – even if it is a little sentimental. But what if, like Ghada Karmi, you cannot fulfil your side of the bargain? The Kudu Project was designed for a *Today* programme lifestyle, and I had signed that blood document promising my wife that he would be my responsibility.

In the event the dog column turned Kudu into part of the solution to my professional dilemmas rather than part of the problem: there was no need to feel guilty about the indulgence of our daily walks once they could, loosely, be defined as research. And, like Alan Furst's Melissa and Ghada Karmi's Rex, Kudu became a literary device.

Except, of course, that he is not a character in a book. He is an individual and very much alive. And that, I very quickly discovered, is what makes writing about him such a pleasure.

The next column is an example of one of those occasions when I set out to use him as a vehicle for describing something else – and then found that he pushed his snout into the copy by the sheer force of his personality. I was exchanging dog emails with one of our neighbours – another convert to dog-ownership in her middle years – and she told me about the stretch of Suffolk coast where she had rented a cottage. It sounded such an intriguing place that I readily accepted the invitation for a picnic and a walk. Writing about Kudu just seemed a good excuse for going somewhere nice and calling it work.

Covehithe proved as beautiful and numinous as promised,

and we had a wonderful walk along the sand. But I remember it as a walk with dogs, not just a walk. There were children there too – and very jolly companions they were – but the dogs defined the day. I might have taken to regarding Kudu as a literary device, but no one had told him about that, so he, of course, continued to act according to his independently minded doggy lights. And the way dogs react to things subtly colours our own experiences.

As the young man at the end of the second column in this chapter discovered, they can also surprise and even change you.

Kudu and his new friend have no sense of history
8 August 2009

The blue waters of the Ionian Sea beckoned. Fingering the tickets, I felt guilty about the Dog: surely he, too, deserved a summer holiday.

It was only a day-trip, and the waters off Suffolk's coast were roiling black, to the eye as thick as tar, but what a walk we had. It is tempting to keep the secret to myself, but this odd slice of our country is resilient against the modern world. A 1930s visitor remarked it 'ambles along at least a century behind the rest of England'.

After two hours in a hot car Kudu showed no

aesthetic interest in the gaunt remains of St Andrew's Church in Covehithe. The graveyard is wild and open, an irresistible invitation to run free, and I am ashamed to admit that I allowed casual canine desecration of several ancient gravestones. But the melancholy oddness of these ruins is a powerful distraction.

Covehithe was a flourishing port during Suffolk's medieval heyday. Its merchants showed off by giving money for church building (Suffolk was called 'sele' or 'holy' on account of its churches); St Andrew's was huge, flaunting six pairs of Gothic windows and a tower tall enough to serve sailors as a landmark. Today there is next to nothing left: no port, no town, and almost no church. Oddest of all is the tiny, hut-like chapel erected in what was once the nave of the great church – one church built inside another, like Russian dolls.

What happened? The dogs – our dog host was a Norfolk Terrier called Alfie, charming in every way, apart from his addiction to horse manure – were more interested in driving history forward than understanding it. Beyond the church there was a path between a field growing some neat but uninspiring East Anglian crop and a low cliff giving on to the beach. As soon as Alfie hit the sand he began to dig, and Kudu copied him. Coastal erosion is one of the reasons for Covehithe's decline – it swallowed the harbour and then the houses; the dogs were determined to make their contribution.

Covehithe's story is a quirky mix of money and faith. The Reformation killed its herring trade, because Protestantism abolished the seventy days of abstinence (which meant eating fish instead of meat) observed in the Old Religion. In the 1640s it received a visit from William 'Smasher' Dowsing, a Taliban-like Puritan charged with the 'destruction of monuments of idolatry and superstition'. Dowsing recorded his acts of iconoclasm with great glee in a journal: at Covehithe church he 'brake down 200 pictures'.

Daniel Defoe, visiting this coast in the early eighteenth century, was inspired to write of 'the fate of things, by which we see that towns, kings, countries, persons have all their elevation, their medium, their declination and even their destruction in the womb of time and the course of nature'. But what are we to make of that tiny chapel, still standing like a defiant gesture amid this desolation of dead dreams?

The beach, stretching all the way to Sizewell, is the kind of landscape one might, in a lazy moment, describe as 'unchanging'. In fact, it has been changing for centuries – and as if to make the point, a bat-like bomber from a nearby airfield made languid circles above us.

But doggy habits never change. Our human hostess was indulgent of Alfie's frantic digging. He is, she pointed out, a terrier (from *terra*, the Latin for earth), designed by humans for precisely this purpose. She conceded it makes him an awkward gardening companion, but how can we blame his atavism?

Kudu's genetic memory was stirred by the wide mere that runs along the beach and is now designated a bird sanctuary. He was in the water like a flash, looking for wildfowl to flush and retrieve. He failed, of course, but – never mind Alfie's manure habit – he stank happily all the way home.

Dogs are not mad – it's the owners who need a shrink
22 August 2009

I have been surprised by the authors who have owned up to dog-curiosity since this column began. In Jermyn Street – the smart shirt place where one still sees pedigree pooches in the shops with titled ladies on their leads – I was approached by a well-known novelist.

Her brother, while breaking up a long relationship, had become concerned about the impact on the family dog, and had taken him to a canine psychiatrist. The shrink told him: 'The dog is fine – but you are in need of professional help.'

In the sixteenth century, long before mad dogs went out in the midday sun with Englishmen, the phrase 'mad dog' meant 'strong ale'. On American campuses it was slang for the hallucinogen PCP. And it has since become a verb in American prisons: if you 'mad dog' a fellow inmate you are eyeballing him. All sorts of odd characters – a Canadian wrestler, a fictional mercenary and a New York talk-show host – have used the 'Mad Dog' sobriquet.

'Dog's gone mad' is a frequent call in Kudu's household. If someone says, 'Go-go-go,' and he dashes down the garden, someone else will shout, 'Dog's gone mad.' The same cry goes up when he turns dervish approaching his favourite pond on Wimbledon Common.

His reactions are entirely logical. The go-go-going is to encourage his pursuit of foxes, and he understands the words so well that even if we whisper them he takes off. He enjoys swimming where he can see the bottom as he walks in, so the Wimbledon pond is preferable to Battersea's formal lake, and the dervish act is natural excitement.

Dogs are grounded and sane; the madness is ours.

The New York writer Reggie Nadelson and I have been corresponding about a dog for her detective hero, Artie Cohen, in her next book (Artie suffered a terrible personal loss in the last one, *Londongrad*, and Reggie thinks a dog might settle him down). I have argued the case for a Springer (I have seen them sniffing for explosives in Afghanistan, and they are perfect police pets), but there is the cultural question of whether a Manhattan dog would need to be lippy – not the Kudu character at all.

Reggie is now dog-obsessed ('on the cusp of dogging', in her words, but I have explained that that is not a nice thing to say over here). She is Jewish, and has sent me details of an agency offering 'Bark Mitzvahs'. 'When outfitting your dog for his Bark Mitzvah,' says the website, 'bear two things in mind: your dog's tolerance for wearing clothes, and your guests' tolerance for seeing dogs in religious garb.' They offer yarmulkes and prayer shawls for dogs, and a 'multi-coloured Star of David dog bandanna', which will 'come in handy for years to come'.

Another well-known woman writer (yes, that is three in this column alone) told me that when she interviewed the Liberal Democrat peer Lord Avebury (he of Orpington by-election fame, for those with long political memories), he declared his intention to leave his body to the abandoned dogs of Battersea Dogs Home, so we can certainly match America in eccentricity.

But there was news this week of a nastier kind of dog-related madness in Britain: our trees (thousands of them, it seems) are being destroyed by what are known as 'weapon dogs' – the owners encourage them to hang from branches to strengthen their jaws. The struggling saplings in the small park where Kudu gets his afternoon walks bear dreadful scars from this habit.

In the queue at Clapham Tesco my wife and stepdaughter found themselves next to a stereo-typical 'weapon dog' owner – but his young Rottweiler was appealingly cuddly and apparently uncorrupted by the tree-biting mentality. They cooed over the puppy until the young man gave way to a smile, enquired after Kudu, and engaged in general dog chat – redeemed for a moment by dog-silliness from dog-related madness.

Snarls all round in a park full of passion
5 September 2009

I have alienated the dog-walkers of Clapham Common: a courteous lady took me gently to task for representing it as a place of fighting-dogs and rough trade. 'We are not all thugs here,' she said. 'We have dogs called Breughel, Rousseau, Shakespeare and' – she indicated a fine-looking Lab – 'Dibley, the lady vicar's dog.'

This week's views may alienate not just my Clapham companions but every bitch-owner in the land. I am plunging into the choppy waters of canine sexual politics.

Kudu, out with my wife in Clapham at the weekend, fixed obsessively on an Alsatian. She was held on a lead by a respectable-looking man, who responded to Kudu's attentions by hitting him with a newspaper (it looked like a Saturday *Telegraph*, putting Kudu in the undignified position of being beaten with his own photograph).

As my wife led him away, she enquired of the Alsatian's owner whether the bitch was on heat. 'None of your business,' he snarled, in a most un-*Telegraph*-reader-like way.

Clapham Common is not a place to pick a fight – especially not with a man ready to use a broadsheet as an offensive weapon. But was it really not her business that he had brought a sexual detonator into the powder keg of a park full of potentially lustful dogs?

A moral conundrum lies at the heart of managing walkies for bitches on heat.

The nub emerged from another difficult exchange – with a young woman enjoying the common accoutred with toddler, Dachshund, picnic and Filipina maid. As Kudu sniffed up in his friendly way, the maid whipped up the Dachshund and held it above her head. Kudu kept leaping at the little dog, despite my forcefully growled instructions.

'She's on heat, I'm afraid,' said the young woman.

Thrown by Kudu's disobedience, I replied, more sharply than I should have done: 'In that case she shouldn't really be out.'

'By that token, nor should he if he's not neutered,' came the reply.

Preposterous logic, surely?

But it has an uncomfortable echo of the argument about dress regularly advanced by my daughter: she believes she should be able to wear whatever she wants without taking responsibility for its impact on men. When I point out that we live in Stockwell rather than Utopia, and suggest a little less leg on a Saturday night, I am accused of sexist piggery.

Male dogs are like sports cars. To enjoy them you have to take pleasure in their flashier qualities – good road handling in wet conditions, a facility for throwing up maximum mud from puddles, and purely theatrical throaty noises. But, like the driver of a fast car, the dog-owner must be absolutely in command – no knocking over children, no foraging in picnics, or paws on white trousers, and absolutely no aggression.

I can now control Kudu in most situations (yes, it was unfortunate when he peed on that

over-dressed Pekinese, but there we are). But I do not
believe I could train him to be calm with a bitch on
heat – the difference, surely, between a dog and a
man. We know of a country Springer whose first
bride arrived on a quad bike; he now becomes
frenzied whenever he hears one.

So – I offer this nervously and after deep
reflection – when owners take bitches into public
places in their season, they have primary responsibility for the behaviour of other dogs, and should not
brandish their newspapers at Spaniels.

But I can also offer them help. In Sweden the
neutering and spaying of dogs used to be outlawed
(as an infringement of doggy rights), so bitch-owners
give them a contraceptive injection like the pill. I
know of one Spaniel owner who uses it here; she
faced fierce resistance from vets, but she is medically
trained and insists the modest health risks are a small
price to pay for the freedom her bitch enjoys courtesy
of her 'chemical *burqa*'.

This piece provoked exactly the kind of vociferous and varied
response I had hoped for. I was accused of sexism ('This is
such a male article') and irresponsibility, and there was something of a hue and cry for Kudu's castration (the very thought
makes me wince and cross my legs). But there was also heavy
website traffic in support of my polemic. The offering I most
enjoyed – for its pithy irascibility – was: 'When your bitch is

on heat you should be responsible enough to keep it away from dogs and not frequent places like Clapham Common, where there is ample sexual activity from humans to keep anyone disgusted.'

At three months into my columnist's life, I was beginning to stretch my legs and march with a swagger – even risking a little experimentation with the form. One week I gave the space to a piece by Kudu himself.

Writing in the persona of your dog is a delicate business, and it is all too easy to overstep the mark. If you asked me whether I know my dog well, I would, of course, say yes, but in truth the characteristics I can identify with anything close to objective certainty are relatively few. He is certainly affectionate (but even aggressive dogs can be affectionate towards their owners), and he seems sensitive to human illness or distress. He is gregarious to the point of social promiscuity, and un-aggressive to the point of wimpishness. I suspect – though this is just a theory – that he has the sort of sunny nature that often goes with good looks: if everyone is always pleased to see you it is bound to incline you towards a benign view of the world.

But beyond that, everything is speculative. Do those deep brown eyes really speak of a certain soulful melancholy? Do the arched eyebrows reflect a baffled concern about the ineffable mysteries of the human world? How does a dog 'think' anyway, and would he recognize an ineffable mystery if he saw one? All these questions are unanswerable, and in trying to imagine a 'voice' for Kudu, I found myself constantly coming up against his essential 'otherness'. If I pushed things too far, I realized, I really would turn him into a two-dimensional literary device.

When the piece was published the *Telegraph* reversed our mug shots, giving him pride of place at the top of the page and consigning me to the foot of the column.

The world beyond this kitchen is so very cruel
19 September 2009

I have – so everyone tells me – expressive eyes, and have found that widening them works wonders with humans; I confess I have in the past exploited their power to solicit a treat or two. But my Master, the wisest of men, has noticed that real melancholy now lies behind them, and he asked me to reflect here on the shame that has come upon my country.

Usually, flopped on the kitchen floor in dreamy anticipation of a plate that needs licking, I enjoy the hour or so of early-evening gossip between Master and Mistress. But last week she brought shocking news from something called the Dogs Trust. There has, it seems, been a record rise in the number of my species being abandoned: 107,228 of us (what can such a monstrous number mean?) were rescued from the streets of this so-called dog-loving nation. She pointed to a headline: 'Big Leap in Stray Dogs as Recession

Bites'. That human appetite for doggy puns be damned! The story told how nearly ten thousand homeless dogs were – in that chilling euphemism – 'put to sleep'.

Once, this would not have worried me: when you are young there are simply too many bottoms to sniff. But my journey to the park takes me past Battersea Dogs Home, and the harrowing howls telling tales of homelessness have become almost too much to bear. Sometimes I meet inmates being walked in the park; one or two are angry – part of the puzzle of life is that some dogs are just not very nice people – but more often they are simply bowed by their misfortunes.

The park brings the gap between rich and poor sharply into focus. All my friends are back with the autumn, greeting one another with Australian kisses (like French ones, but down under) and telling tales of exotic holidays – there are two terriers who spent a seaside summer on the Isle of Wight, and one flirty young bitch with a collar-bell claims to have flown to Tuscany. I live less glamorously than the Chelsea Set and, of course, have my complaints: why, for example, does my Master root out my carefully hidden bones just as they reach delicious maggoty maturity? But we are all so much more fortunate than our abandoned brothers and sisters.

We are, of course, all pedigree and, yes, I do take pride in the fifteen Field Champions I count among my great-great-grandparents; my mother, Madeline of Meadowlea (her Kennel Club name), was born of the champion Springer Steadroc Sker and Miss Tickle, no less. But now that my social conscience has been pricked, I wonder a little about this obsession with breeding. There is a Battersea regular whose mistress introduces him, with a flamboyant French flourish, as a 'Boar-hunting Grand Basset Griffon Vendéen'; he is a nice enough fellow, but how many boars are there in Battersea? And my Master recently brought news to dinner of a Labour peer buying a 'Madagascan Coton de Tuléar'. Can we really tolerate such frivolity on the Left?

All sorts of distressing news drifts down from the kitchen table: thousands of dogs have been clubbed to death in China because of a rabies scare, and a Danish MP wants to cull every one of his country's mongrels to eliminate aggressive genes from the pool. How can the world beyond this comfortable kitchen be such a cruel place? There was a time when we could look down on these brute foreigners and their dog-phobic ways, but I wonder if that is really still so?

Perhaps I should drop the 'English' from my name and become simply a 'Springer Spaniel'.

I shall not often have a public voice of this kind. May I add a personal message? I understand from my

Master that my sister Mielie is not well, having eaten a plate of sausages with the cocktail sticks still attached; I wish her a full recovery.

3

The Humanness of Dogs

A sixth sense, or just howling at the moon?
3 October 2009

I HAVE RECEIVED AN affecting letter from a reader, which I quote, minus a couple of identifying details, with his permission.

In 1984 my first wife was dying in hospital, and my son and I took it in turns to spend time with her. Our dog, a super Welsh Springer Spaniel, would not sleep in the kitchen while she was away, he insisted on sleeping in either my bedroom or my son's. My wife died when I was at the hospital. At 3.30 a.m., I phoned my son. 'I know Mum died at three o'clock,' he said. 'Basil got up and howled.' It was the only time in his fourteen years he did so.

My correspondent wondered whether other readers might offer stories of canine 'sixth sense'.

I take Hamlet's view: 'There are more things in Heaven and Earth,' he tells his rationalist friend Horatio after the Ghost appears, 'than are dreamt of in your philosophy.' An openness to such stories seems saner than a Dawkins-esque broadside against science-denying sentimentality. But researching the relevant literature has tilted me in the Dawkins direction: this story is from an American collection called *Angel Dogs*.

The narrator, a retired marine, is walking his Jack Russell in a cemetery. I am afraid he has called the dog Corporal J.R. and given him his service number, USMC 21264539. We soon know that he might be a tiresome walking companion: 'I always carry water, collapsible water bowl for J.R., J.R.'s first aid kit, a Swiss Army knife, a snack for both of us, my bird identification manual and my trusty Nikon 7x5 binoculars.'

J.R. suddenly begins digging frantically, and our hero notices that the dog is uncovering a military grave. He helps shift the debris and . . . 'My heart pounded as I read the inscription: "Jack A Russell,

Texas, Cpl, Signals Corps, 1928–1952".' Our man describes how 'Corporal J.R. laid his head on the headstone of Corporal Jack Russell, a soldier with his own name who was killed in the Korean War,' and declares, 'I continue to marvel how a little dog paid honour and respect by bringing new meaning to the belief that no soldier should ever be forgotten.'

There is also a tale of an Arizona man whose religious confidence is restored when Temujin, his Mastiff, leads him to an abandoned baseball cap carrying the legend 'No Fear'. I have lived in America and am a diehard Yankophile, but really!

The commonest evidence of dog sixth sense is finding an eager animal waiting in the hall when we turn the door key. Kudu does this act terribly well, thumping his tail and, like the gun-dog he was bred to be, bringing a shoe as a welcome (he has a good soft mouth and, an incident involving a pair of Jimmy Choos belonging to a son's girlfriend notwithstanding, the footwear usually survives).

Here I definitely favour the rationalist explanation. I work at home, and often see the build-up to this performance behind the scenes: Kudu is just as excited when the postman approaches the front steps as he is in the moments before one of the family walks in. There is some science around about this, and it suggests that dogs have extremely sensitive hearing – a faculty that may also explain the well-attested cases (the first was recorded in Greece in the fourth century BC) of dogs becoming agitated before earthquakes.

And then, as I mulled on the evidence for this column, my eighty-seven-year-old father-in-law came to stay, recovering from an infection. He was still weak, and had a couple of bad shivering bouts – Kudu immediately went into a severe fit of sympathetic whimpering. When the invalid retired to bed, the Dog accompanied him and spent hours keeping a watchful eye on his condition until he felt well.

A sixth sense or acute sensitivity? It does not really matter what you call it, does it?

This column provoked one of the most intriguing and amusing reader responses I have had. Checking the *Telegraph* Opinion website after the piece was published, I found the following story from someone called Craig:

Some years ago, my friend had a black Labrador. He lived in a downstairs maisonette in London. It was an ordinary dog – friendly, well behaved and not particularly remarkable although obviously intelligent. My friend was divorced and lonely and the dog and I were his only real friends.

On this particular occasion, we were sitting in his lounge and discussing women. He said that he had given up on dating agencies and lonely hearts ads and couldn't meet anyone. The dog was in the room and I suppose 'listening'. I remember the dog was there because he always sat at my feet when I came around. After a while, my friend said to the dog: 'Merlin, find me a perfect woman, will you?' and we both laughed. Minutes later we were in his kitchenette making a coffee when he heard Merlin barking really loudly in the front garden which he had accessed from the backyard. 'Probably someone at the door,' I said.

We went to the front door and opened it and Merlin was standing next to a truly stunning-looking woman and barking. She said, 'Hallo, is this your dog? He just jumped into my car as I opened the door to go . . . I have been visiting someone a few doors along!' We stood there staring and dumbfounded.

My friend Chris married Stunning-Sarah eighteen months later.

I would love to know whether Chris and Stunning-Sarah lived happily ever after, and whether the magician-dog Merlin cast any more such happy spells on his master's life. Craig (or Chris or Stunning-Sarah), if by some extraordinary piece of serendipity, you chance to read this, do please get in touch.

Marshall McLuhan, the high-priest of modern media theory, famously described television as a 'cool medium' and radio as a 'hot' one. When I worked on television I found that the screen put a certain distance between me and the audience: people sometimes treated me as if I was not quite real. Radio is very different: listeners feel a much more intimate connection with the voices that come into their bedrooms and bathrooms, and they are often surprisingly uninhibited about berating or praising you for what they have heard you say.

But a column is, I have discovered, even 'hotter': readers take what you write very personally indeed. I got into terrible trouble for the column on Covehithe (see pages 40–43): my flippant comment about allowing the 'casual canine desecration of several ancient gravestones' did not go down at all well, and a local landowner tracked me down through my agents with a furious letter. I had to write her an abject apology, and it was upsetting because I really had thought Covehithe to be a magical place. It was a good lesson in the importance of weighing words carefully.

For the most part, however, I have found the sense of a very direct relationship with readers a rewarding one. Most of the feedback reached me through the paper's website, where readers are encouraged to express their views. The blogosphere is a wild and violent place: people seem to feel released from the sort of conventions that would inhibit them if they were writing for the printed page (I was once described as 'a symptom of the moral degeneracy of modern Britain' in the blog of a writer who would certainly never have said such a thing in her national newspaper column). But dog-owners are, by and large, gentle folk, and there has been remarkably little abuse.

Some people simply have odd or eccentric dog jokes they want to share with a wider audience. Thus this: 'My uncle had a dog named Bob. This was so spooky since everyone knows that normally Bob's your uncle! In fact my uncle was named Arthur.'

And there has been a fairly steady flow of good dog stories, some of which I incorporated into columns, some of which I just chuckled over, or shared with my family. The column became a conversation.

Know thy President by his choice of pooch
17 October 2009

It is a journalistic commonplace that 'dog bites man' is not a story, but 'man bites dog' absolutely is. But try this: dog bites ex-president as punishment for moving him out of a palace with one of the most desirable gardens in the world.

The facts are these. Jacques Chirac's miniature Maltese Terrier, Sumo, had to be treated for mental health problems after leaving the Élysée and its glorious stretch of lawn. The Chiracs now live in a huge flat, courtesy of the late Lebanese prime minister Rafik Hariri (imagine what this newspaper would make of a similar arrangement for one of our ex-prime ministers), but this is apparently not grand enough for Sumo. He began 'routinely' assaulting his master, and recently savaged Monsieur Chirac's stomach, causing great distress to Madame Chirac: 'I was extremely frightened by all the blood,' she said. 'It's awful, those little teeth!' Sumo has been sent to the country in disgrace.

For a dog columnist with an interest in international politics and a spell as Paris correspondent on the CV, this is as close as it gets to the perfect news story. Politics, the French culture of public life and the impenetrable oddness of the French doggy mind, all these things suggest themselves for comment. What riches for rumination during the walks on this week's glorious autumn days! And I think that Kudu and I have reached a similar conclusion – although we approach the matter from different angles.

My instinct is that to mine a moral from the story we should begin with the politics. And here is a spooky thing: George W. Bush's Scottish Terrier Barney became a biter during his last days at the White House too. Could it be that unsuccessful presidents make bad dog-owners?

All dog-owners know that their hounds can pick up their moods, and Barney's victims were members of the press corps. A Reuters correspondent tried to give him a pat a few days after the Republican defeat in the presidential election, and Barney gave him a nasty nip in the finger. Is it too fanciful to suggest that he was fulfilling his master's private fantasies?

Kudu looks at the dog first and the master second, and I have a shrewd idea that the Sumo and Barney stories would confirm one of his prejudices: I realize this is by far and away the most controversial statement this column has ever ventured, but I am beginning to suspect he disapproves of small dogs.

We passed a woman on Clapham Common carrying a diminutive pooch like a baby in a papoose. Kudu did not growl – he has extremely good manners – but he fired a look of bemused disdain at the thing. What, after all, is the point of a walk if you cannot run constantly in circles on the important business of picking up smells, pausing only to roll in fox poo from time to time?

Kudu may be on to something here: is a very small dog appropriate for a man in power? Vladimir Putin apparently thought not, and once told George Bush that a Scottish Terrier was beneath the dignity of a world leader, boasting that his own Labrador was 'bigger, tougher, stronger, faster, meaner' than the American First Dog. This took place before Barney's savaging of the White House press corps, of course, and you can see where Mr Putin is coming from. But what sort of a politician thinks being mean is something to take pride in?

Whether you look at the dog first or the man first, the principle is the same: you will know one if you know the other. And while party politics is not the business of the column, that is not a bad way to judge a leader.

Oh, and I have a sense of where David Cameron stands on the dog thing, because of something he let slip in the studio. But I am keeping schtum.

Cameron told me – I think during Thought for the Day – that he had once owned a Springer. At the time I worried that revealing this fact might have listeners pricking up their ears for any hint of a Tory bias in my broadcasting. He also warned me that they get smelly when they are old; we have not got there yet, but I suspect he is probably right.

Join a US Howl-oween Parade? No thanks . . .
31 October 2009

Restless on the Amtrak from Washington to New York, I made my way to the dining car. We were skimming the open reaches of water along the Delaware coast and, as I admired the handsome houses with their lawns down to moorings on the sound, I fell in with a couple of Wall Street types heading home.

The collars were open, the silk ties at half-mast, the tailored suits a little rumpled, and they were lining up the beers. We talked escrow, liquidity and leverage. I shook my head sympathetically about the search for a zero-plus position, wondered how long the numbers would stack and went over the wall with them on a couple of deals. It was like being in a Spielberg movie – as America so often is: one of these guys, I thought, will get home and find an alien in the tool shed.

The man in Institutional Risk Analysis – ho-ho, I hear you say – suddenly turned sentimental: 'Can't wait to get back to Westchester,' he said, 'and have a good romp with my Westie in the yard!' He and his fellow Master of the Universe then talked dogs all the way through New Jersey with as much enthusiasm as they had shown for high finance.

Travelling the United States with a dog column-ist's eye for the first time, I was struck by the way its dog cultures vary. Washington is an easy-going place with a southern culture of politesse: its dogs conform perfectly to its ethos, appearing for a leisurely amble along its wide, tree-lined streets twice daily, never pulling on their leads (unlike a certain person I could mention) and greeting one another with polite reserve. Most of the dogs I encountered in New York, by contrast, were like my hotel room there: tiny and ludicrously 'designer'. And in the über-hip Californian workspace of the Google-plex (where, in a perfect Californian moment, I witnessed one of the Internet giant's legendary founders roller-blading through Reception carrying his lunch) they have an open dog policy – the hounds mingle happily with the geeks 'writing code'.

America knocks our claim to be a dog-loving country into the proverbial cocked hat.

In the United States, if you want a partner who shares your doggy enthusiasms, there is a special singles agency (www.datemypet.com, if you are interested). If it is dog news you are after, the *New York Post* has a weekly page – with features on such matters as Canine Acupuncture. *Modern Dog* magazine can tell you where to find the Top Ten Dog Blogs. And if you are facing doggy bereavement, how about a 'memorial pillow', which allows you to 'conceal the ashes in a discreet interior pouch so you can hold them close'?

The bookshops in Washington and New York are stuffed with titles like *Come Back Como; winning the heart of a reluctant dog*. Redemption by doggy affection is usually the theme: the blurb for *A Big Little Life – Memoir of a Joyful Dog* tells how Trixie 'taught Dean [Koontz, the writer] to trust his instincts, persuaded him to cut down to a fifty-hour work week, and, perhaps most important, renewed in him a sense of wonder . . .'

It would be dangerous for this column to sneer – I have done my fair share of anthropomorphizing on my Kudu adventures. But sentimentality slips very easily into cruelty. This season in the United States is marked by what are known as Howl-oween Parades, for which dogs are given absurd and demeaning costumes. Would I dress Kudu in a pink tutu? Or put him in a French maid's outfit? I would not, and I worry about the dog ethics of those who would.

And it is very nice to be home. Kudu and I do not really do 'romps in the yard', but we do enjoy sniffing around the garden together, working out what needs attention with the secateurs.

Every dog should have his day at the workplace
14 November 2009

Kudu and I offer belated congratulations to Molly, a Welsh Springer Spaniel of our acquaintance, who has been named Westminster Dog of the Year. Her owner, the shadow international development secretary Andrew Mitchell, was said to be 'overwhelmed', and declared that he and Molly were 'collecting the award on behalf of all dogs in Sutton Coldfield' (his constituency). In this newspaper's photograph of the event, Molly herself, gloriously confident in her beauty, looked as if she would have little truck with such shameless political opportunism.

Young beauties can be powerful role models, and in her private life Molly provides a socially valuable example: she is a working dog. I do not mean she picks up pheasants or herds sheep; far less am I using the phrase in the sense of 'working girl' (I happen to know that her chastity is a closely guarded treasure, because I have enquired on Kudu's behalf). Molly is taken to work by her mistress.

I reported in my last column that the Internet giant Google includes an open dog policy in the trendy working practices (volleyball at lunchtime, slogans like 'You don't have to wear a suit to be serious' and so on) it deploys to encourage creativity. The time has come for this column to take a Public Position: dogs in the workplace should be encouraged as widely as possible.

Some businesses can be given exemptions: you would not want Kudu's wag in a glass factory, and I can see the need for the 'Sorry, no dogs – not even cute ones' sign, which has recently appeared in our local butcher (they make up for it by being very generous with bones). But the general presumption should be that dogs are allowed to come to work with their owners.

Employers would quickly appreciate the impact on staff relations. It is impossible to have an argument in the presence of a dog – certainly a nicely brought-up one. If anyone in our household speaks with a raised voice, Kudu adopts an expression of distress, and politely intervenes.

Dogs aid concentration: if I have something diffi-cult to write I retreat to my shed, and with Kudu at my feet, the words come easily. Dogs have sharp instincts for health and safety: if I work for too long at a stretch I find a large head nuzzling my knees, demanding a screen break.

Above all, dogs can puncture the pomposity that is such a common feature of corporate life. There is a famous passage about this in Pepys's account of the return of Charles II to England in 1660. The king arrived at Dover in great splendour aboard the *Royal Charles*, and Pepys was in the flotilla of small boats that accompanied him: 'I went, and Mr Mansell, and one of the King's footmen,' he recorded, 'with a dog that the king loved (which shit in the boat, which made us laugh, and me think that a king and all that belong to him are but just as others are).' Obviously one would hope to avoid the shitting, but the cheer-fully egalitarian manner with which dogs treat humans would remind the grandest CEO that he is 'just as others are'.

By way of a postscript to the launch of this important campaign, here is a charming story a reader has offered in response to my column on a canine 'sixth sense'. He described looking after an elderly and unwell father who was subject to what he termed 'fits' towards the end of his life, and he wrote that his West Highland Terrier, Sophie, always warned him in advance that a fitting episode was about to take place. She would approach the bedside and bark in a particular way, enabling my correspondent to offer comfort when it was needed.

Imagine what a dog like that could do in the board room.

My stint as ITN's diplomatic editor in the early 1990s coincided with a period of especially intense international summitry. The Soviet empire was collapsing, Germany was being reunited, the Balkans were in flames, and the European Union (or the European Community, as it then was) was convulsed by negotiations over what would become the euro. All of these things required seemingly endless meetings of Very Important Persons, and it was my job to cover them. I spent a punishing amount of time getting on planes and living in hotel rooms.

Most of these meetings took place in glamorous surroundings – a palace in Rome, a château in the French countryside or, famously, the picturesque old Dutch town of Maastricht – but the way they were run made it quite impossible to appreciate or enjoy the places. The host government would find some suitably utilitarian space – very often an underground car park – where they could erect a 'media village' of temporary offices and broadcasting facilities, and these artificial worlds became our homes; we could attend press conferences, eat our meals and put together our stories without ever coming up for air. I used to arrive early in the morning and leave late (*News at Ten* was my main duty), and it was perfectly possible to spend a couple of days in Paris, Moscow or Washington without seeing anything at all of those great cities. It became a blur: they were years of going everywhere but visiting nowhere – and any reader who travels for business will recognize the experience.

I have vowed never to travel like that again – in fact, I have become primly moralistic on the subject. If you find yourself somewhere exotic at someone else's expense, having stomped down a great big carbon footprint to get there, I think you have a duty to explore the place a bit. No matter how exhausted I am at the end of a news-reporting trip, I always force myself to look around.

And Kudu gave me a new way of getting under the skin (or should that be the coat?) of new places.

The autumn of 2009 was another period of intense travel: I was working on a radio series about the decade of the 'noughties', and we had ambitiously set ourselves the task of telling the story with a global sweep. We were trying to do big-picture history to a news-style deadline, and the pace was frantic. At the same time I was working to the gentler but still insistent rhythm of these fortnightly columns.

So I looked for material whenever and wherever I could find it: I read the papers in a different way, watched people in the streets in a different way, and talked to them differently too. Interviews for news and current affairs broadcasting are a quest for the essential: you dig your way through self-serving spin and drill down to a few diamonds of truly consequential information. Dog-watching is the reverse: the inconsequential is everything. You are on the prowl for the odd and unexpected, a moment (like the banditry of the badly behaved street dog in the next column) that will spark an idea.

And by the time I found what I wanted I had usually learnt to see the character and habits of a place in a new and fuller way. When you do not quite know what you are looking for you have to get your nose out of your notebook and watch the world go by – and that is when travel really does broaden the mind.

Wish you were here – though not on the menu
28 November 2009

Ruijin Guesthouse
Shanghai

Dear Kudu,

There was a picture in my *Shanghai Daily* this morning of a demobilized young Chinese soldier bidding farewell to his sniffer dog; it looked uncannily like you – with the soulful eyes and its human-like hugging – and the picture prompted me to write with an apology.

The two things you hate most are cufflinks and suitcases: the cufflinks tell you I am going to work, and the suitcase means one of us is going away, a practice of which you heartily disapprove. I am sceptical about the Slough of Despond into which you sink, because I know what fun you have with the lady who walks you. But I concede that California, Bosnia, the Netherlands and China within a month is a bit much, and I have missed our walks.

But you would be amazed by what is happening here. Take this headline in the *China Daily*: 'Pet lovers save 800 cats from dinner table'. Do not pass this on to Ruff and Tumble – I know they are cats but we share the same household. And I have to tell you that in China people eat dogs too. I spotted a clever-looking mongrel pinching a lump of meat from a pavement grill, and, as it disappeared into the crowd amid curses, my Chinese assistant exclaimed, 'I do hope it is not eating a relation.'

The *China Daily* reported that a group of pet lovers had picketed the cat trader's premises in Tianjin until he opened his rows and rows of iron cages. The trader said he had paid ten yuan (a pound) for each of them, and was quite open about the fact that they were to be 'slaughtered and served as food' in Guangzhou. Since there is no law against cat trading in China, the only weapon the concerned citizens could deploy was moral suasion – and they won.

Chairman Mao, Communist China's founder, condemned pets as a decadent bourgeois distraction. And just as China's citizens have had to live with its one-child policy, many Chinese cities now have a one-dog policy. The cost of a dog-licence can be exorbitant: in Shanghai it is as much as two hundred pounds a year if you want to keep a dog in the city centre.

But as China has become richer, more of its people have turned to the pleasures of dog-ownership. Today there are a hundred and fifty thousand registered dogs in Shanghai alone – and, locals tell me, many more without a licence. This September a Tibetan Mastiff called Yangtze River Number Two became the most expensive dog in history – bought for £350,000 by a woman from Shaanxi.

As you and I know – and the Tianjin cat trader discovered to his cost – pet-owners can organize when the call comes. Do you remember the day we found an elderly Dachshund loose in Battersea Park? Within minutes we had collected a posse of Chelsea ladies to catch the poor fellow and deliver him to the Parks Police. There was a thrilling sense of shared purpose that made us all friends for a while – indeed, one lady took things rather too far by telling me about the ghastliness of her sister-in-law ('the sort of woman who couldn't manage a wet dog').

China's dog-owners are being inspired to action in just the same way. This summer, lawmakers in Shanghai debated a draconian new code to ban dogs from city centre public places and even from lifts – a significant step in a city of skyscrapers. The proposals provoked furious public debate – of a kind you do not often see here. And peaceful non-political protest like this – an association of citizens sharing a common purpose – can be the most serious of threats to an authoritarian regime.

So Mao was right, Kudu, you are a manifestation of bourgeois decadence. But hurrah for that, I say.

Home soon,

Your Master

4

The Dogginess of Dogs

MY DAUGHTER'S BOYFRIEND, Andrew, came back from Afghanistan on leave in late November 2009, and his description of his duties in the Musa Qaleh district of Helmand Province was hair-raising.

He was commanding a forward reconnaissance unit, which meant (this is my very un-military gloss on his explanation) taking his men into an unclaimed piece of desert and waiting for a few days to see whether anyone shot at them. Quite often they did – unsurprisingly, really, given that the Taliban had been harassing troops around Musa Qaleh ever since it was retaken by the British in December 2007. The dog story he told me was, of course, a gift for the dog column, but it was also a revealing insight into the fighting in Afghanistan.

By this stage of the war we had already become – sadly –

all too familiar with the scenes of those coffins draped with the Union Flag arriving at RAF Lyneham, and being driven in dignified silence through crowded streets in the Wiltshire town of Wootton Bassett. But the degree to which bullets and bombs had become almost routine in the lives of front-line soldiers in Afghanistan still had not come fully home to people in Britain.

Those doing the front-line fighting are often shockingly young. I did a reporting stint in Helmand in 2008, and a couple of my eldest son's school contemporaries introduced themselves to me in the British base at Lashkar Gah; my first instinct – imagining with horror my son being entrusted with an offensive weapon – was to tell them they were far too young to be playing with guns, and could they please put them down at once. They were, in fact, twenty-five, and therefore already veterans with – to me – dauntingly heavy responsibilities.

The Afghan campaign has done something very odd to the make-up of the armed forces. The senior officers – of my age – joined up in the more peaceful days of Cold War soldiering, and some of them have reached the top with relatively little or no experience of what it feels like to be shot at. The majority of those at the bottom, however, know that feeling all too well: there is now a whole generation of service personnel who have been through combat, often of a very bloody kind.

Andrew's dog story brings some of that home. Had it not been for the dog factor, it would simply have been another day in the routine of fighting – 'kinetic activity', as soldiers like to call it – and would never have been considered worthy of note in a national newspaper. The story also evokes the cheeriness these young troops somehow manage to maintain in such high-stress circumstances. Andrew later told me that he read the piece to his men, which I found moving.

Derring-do of our Afghan hounds
12 December 2009

Kudu has recently been failing in his main contribution to the happiness of the household: offering extravagant welcome to family and favoured friends.

When I got home late this week he did no more than poke his nose round the kitchen door, then slipped off to settle back to sleep – on my side of the bed, if you please. Worse still, he let me down during a media opportunity. The *Today* programme is preparing a Christmas report on that endlessly intriguing question of whether dogs can sense when people are coming home, and the desk sent an ace reporter down to wait with me for the moment when my stepdaughter would arrive back from school. Kudu stiffened and stared at the front door in a promising way – and then got so caught up in a love-in with one of the cats that he missed the critical moment altogether.

But I am happy to say that he laid on the full works – frantic racing around the hall, offering of a well-chewed sock in lieu of dead pheasant, etc. –

when my daughter's boyfriend came to see us on leave from serving in Afghanistan. This was just as well, as the daughter's boyfriend (DB, as I shall call him for reasons of operational security) had been sticking up for Kudu's species in very difficult circumstances.

DB's unit employs an explosives sniffer dog – an English Springer like Kudu. He tested its effectiveness by burying a hand grenade in the sand, and in no time at all Kudu's cousin (I am sure, since all the decent ones are related) was stock still on his haunches with his nose quivering in the right direction. DB also uses the dog to break the ice with Afghans he meets: he is often operating in areas where people have never encountered foreign troops before, and they are fascinated by the relationship between a well-trained dog and its handlers.

He described to us a joint operation he had conducted with a group of British troops from what is known as the OMLeT – more properly, the Operational Mentoring and Liaison Team, who are training the Afghan National Army. While DB's armoured vehicles were struggling across a ploughed field, they ran into an ambush and came under fire from the Taliban. They managed to reach a commanding position on a ridge, and once they had suppressed the fire against them, the OMLeT and their Afghan comrades withdrew.

But the terrain dictated that the only way out for DB's unit was to re-cross the area where they had come under attack (a.k.a. 'the kill zone'). Halfway over the field one of the vehicles got bogged down in the mud, and as they were trying to tow it out they came under Taliban fire again. It was at this point that a message came across the radio from the OMLeT: they had had their pregnant pet dog with them and it had got lost in the withdrawal; would DB and his troops very much mind rescuing her?

Amazingly, they managed to find her: Sandy (not her real name, operational security again) was whimpering (unsurprisingly) in the middle of the battlefield, so they scooped her up and took her home. But the poor thing was so traumatized that she miscarried in the armoured vehicle. When they delivered her back, the Afghan troops thought the whole episode richly and darkly comic; the Brits in the OMLeT, by contrast, were upset about losing the puppies.

We are lucky to live well enough to keep dogs for pleasure. Life in a place like Helmand does not allow the indulgences of our dog culture; there you own a dog to guard your property and protect your person. Our soldiers are trying to fight and offer an example at the same time, and, in the words of Immanuel Kant (not a man much read in Taliban circles, I suspect), 'We can judge the heart of a man by his treatment of animals.'

We should take our lead from Lord Byron
Boxing Day 2009

Kudu is spending part of the holidays near Newstead Abbey, the old home of the Byron family. Newstead now belongs to the Nottingham Corporation and (the poet would not have approved) can be hired for corporate events. But the gaunt remains of the twelfth-century Augustinian priory still stand, and the vast grounds, with their woods and lakes, are as romantic as ever. What better Christmas present for a dog than a few wet walks in wild weather?

We will visit the memorial to Boatswain, Lord Byron's famously gentle Newfoundland, who died of rabies in 1808. This impressive structure – topped with a marble urn – is inscribed with perhaps the best dog epitaph ever written.

> Near this spot
> Are deposited the Remains of one
> Who possessed Beauty without Vanity
> Strength without Insolence,
> Courage without Ferocity
> And all the Virtues of Man without his Vices.
> This Praise, which would be unmeaning
>   Flattery
> If inscribed over human ashes,
> Is but a just tribute to the Memory of
> BOATSWAIN, a Dog.

Though widely attributed to Byron himself, it now seems these lines were written by his Cambridge friend John Hobhouse. Hobhouse might have been trying to tease the poet, who had Vanity, Insolence, Ferocity and Vices in spades.

Boatswain died when Byron was in his most Gothic phase. He had the skull of a long-dead monk mounted as a drinking cup ('In me behold the only skull/From which, unlike a living head/Whatever flows is never dull', read the inscription), and one nineteenth-century memoir records that 'He invited his friends to orgies, where he had an ox in imitation of the ancient Homeric banquets, where he made libations of wine as in Asiatic festivals, where they wrestled and fought like Roman gladiators, concluding with scenes of riot and debauchery.'

But there seems no doubt about Byron's grief for Boatswain. Another friend recorded that 'He more than once, with his bare hand, wiped away the slather from the dog's lips during the paroxysms.' And Byron wrote that his dog died, 'retaining all the gentleness of his nature to the end, never attempting to do the least injury to anyone near him'.

Byron's affection for animals in general and dogs in particular is one of the most unexpected leitmotivs of his life. His famous acquisition of a bear at Trinity College, Cambridge, arose from an argument over his bulldog, Smut: informed that the rules allowed no dogs in college, he bought the bear (not covered by the rules) to taunt the Fellows.

When Shelley visited Byron in Ravenna in 1821 he found 'eight enormous dogs, three monkeys, five cats, an eagle, a crow, and a falcon' roaming Byron's house. And when Byron's body was shipped home after his death in Greece, Hobhouse found another faithful Newfoundland lying at the foot of the coffin.

Why this sentimentality in a man who was 'mad, bad and dangerous to know'? The question is pertinent at this season because, when the snow blows and the wind howls, all dog-owners must ask why they submit themselves to the discipline of the daily walk. The complaint 'Doggies are a bore, they never close the door' rings especially true when open doors let in freezing blasts.

The answer surely lies in the uncomplicated nature of dog emotions: the simplicity of their pleasures, the transparency of their transgressions (we caught Kudu begging under the table, and the briefest grunt sent him slinking off in embarrassment). The more complicated the life, the more appealing this simplicity becomes – and Byron's life was nothing if not complicated.

Last weekend I watched Kudu putting up pheasants, utterly absorbed in what his genes were telling him, delighting in the exercise of nose and limbs. It had been a complicated week of deadlines and juggled appointments; not quite the same as a Homeric orgy, but I think – in a phrase the poet would never have used – I know where Byron was coming from.

Dogs were still a source of controversy at Trinity College when I came up as an undergraduate 170 years after Byron bought his bear. The Master was R. A. B. Butler, the famously clever and grand Tory politician who should – he thought, anyway – have been prime minister, but was stitched up by Macmillan. His formidable wife Mollie brought a small terrier with her when they moved into the Master's Lodge, and Lady Butler was not someone accustomed to being told she was not allowed to do things.

Rather than rewriting the ancient anti-dog statutes, the college authorities decided to reassign her pet's species. An undergraduate who spotted the terrier in Great Court rather cheekily brought it to the attention of one of the college porters (never without their intimidating bowler hats, the porters were responsible for enforcing college discipline). 'That, sir,' he was told, 'is not a dog – College Regulations do not permit that. That is a cat.'

Trust the good book to give a dog a bad name

9 January 2010

Jerusalem is not a doggy city; when I return there next week (on Radio 4 duties) I do not expect Spaniels in the throng at Damascus Gate.

There have been doggy episodes in its long past. The Crusaders brought their hunting hounds (think of the stone dogs on Crusader tombs), and dog stories feature in accounts of the British Mandate period. But the city has its alchemy for managing foreign cultures: it absorbs the bits that suit it, and shakes off those that sit uneasily with its soul. Its doglessness is true to its Biblical roots.

Dogs get a bad press in the Bible. Brewer (of *Phrase and Fable*) notes that 'There is no expression in the Bible of the fidelity, love and watchful care of the dog, so highly honoured by ourselves.' Instead dogs are represented as debased and worthless creatures.

In the First Book of Kings, dogs are used to curse Jeroboam, the errant leader of the Israelites who persuades his people to worship two golden calves. Jeroboam receives this prophetic warning: 'Thus says the Lord ... I will ... consume the house of Jeroboam, just as one burns up dung until it is all gone. Anyone belonging to Jeroboam who dies in the city the dogs shall eat.'

It is the same in the New Testament. The Second Letter of Peter explicitly links dogs with that most unclean of animals, the pig. Of apostates the writer declares, 'It has happened to them according to the true proverb, "The dog turns back to its own vomit," and "The sow is washed only to wallow in the mud".'

The post-walk towelling of Kudu this winter has left me puzzled by this Biblical view of dogs as unclean. The goats in Bedouin settlements outside Jerusalem may be a little dusty, but the writers of 1 Kings and 2 Peter surely never encountered anything remotely like a Spaniel back from a ramble in the English countryside.

Kudu has recently been walked in North Yorkshire, Nottinghamshire and on the Surrey Downs. The pattern is always the same. First he gets wet and looks bedraggled. Then he acquires a long bramble in his bottom fur, and races around like one of those military jeeps with floppy aerials waving wildly from the rear end. Then he finds a fetid puddle and sinks his legs and tummy down as far as they will go. Then we (my wife usually, if I am honest) rub him down in an affectionate way, as if all this is somehow endearing.

Surely we, not those who gave us the Bible, should be hurling imprecations at this wilful wallowing in filth.

The clue to this conundrum may lie in the writings of St Paul. There is a famous passage where Paul condemns the practice of circumcision – it is controversial as well as famous because it is cited as a foundation of Christian anti-Semitism. 'Beware of the dogs,' writes the Apostle to the Gentiles, 'beware of the evil workers, beware of those who mutilate the flesh.'

Paul is using 'dogs' as a metaphor for false teachers who are preaching a perverted Christian message. He has taken the very thing we modern British dog-walkers value – the human-like qualities of our pets – and turned them into something sinister. We look at dogs and see the best of ourselves reflected back (those dogs on Crusader tombs were an artistic shorthand for fidelity to God) while the writers of the Bible seem to have seen something witch-like: 'Outside are the dogs and sorcerers and fornicators and murderers and idolaters,' declares the Book of Revelation.

Enough of this speculative persiflage. Here is a practical question by way of a postscript. Kudu's fur has a remarkable self-cleaning quality. Leave him in the kitchen for a while, and, no matter how mired in filth he has been, his coat restores itself to its lustrous chocolate and milk. Can any reader explain how this happens?

The Bible is, notoriously, one of those subjects that 'gets them going'. This column was picked up by an American 'ideas website' as a news story, and it produced a gratifyingly heavy level of traffic. There were anti-religious dog-lovers ('Screw the Bible and all those who hate dogs!'), and anti-dog religious enthusiasts ('I can't wait for a heaven with no dogs barking and no dog sh*t on the pavement'). But there were also good Bible-believing Christians who loved dogs, and tried to persuade me I had got it wrong.

Some of them quoted the story of the Woman of Canaan, who approaches Jesus asking him to cast a devil out of her daughter. He initially turns her away because she is a Gentile: 'I was sent only to the lost sheep of the lands of Israel,' he says, in the Matthew version of the story, and when she persists he delivers a punchy one-liner: 'It is not fair to take the children's food and throw it to the dogs.' But she comes back, quick as a flash: 'Yes, Lord, yet even the dogs eat the food that falls from their masters' table.' Jesus is so impressed with this riposte that he grants her wish.

This is an attractive story because it shows Jesus reacting well to a clever woman, not, it would appear, in the least put out by her cheek. But quite how you can use it to suggest that he was a dog-lover I fail to see: he plainly uses the 'dogs' as an insult, in keeping with the great Biblical tradition.

I do not want to make too much of the story of Sandy the Afghan mongrel, but her sad fate does seem to me symptomatic of the difficulty we Brits have in understanding Afghan culture.

And not long after this next column was published we were given a sharp reminder that, no matter how regular the battles in Afghanistan, they can never really be 'routine' for those involved. Andrew, my source for Afghan dog stories, was seriously injured when his armoured vehicle overturned while chasing a suspect car in the desert; he was thrown clear but damaged his spine and crushed a knee on impact. At the time of writing he is walking again (which did not seem at all certain when we first saw him in Selly Oak Hospital nine months ago) but still has a long way to go.

Unhappy ending for one dog of war
23 January 2010

I reported recently the story of Sandy, a mongrel adopted by British troops training the Afghan National Army in Helmand; heavily pregnant, she was rescued from a battlefield by a unit under the command of my daughter's boyfriend, and although she miscarried – not unnaturally, in the circumstances – she survived the fire-fight.

Sandy subsequently surprised everyone by giving birth to one healthy puppy, and I had hopes that the story would have a happy ending. I have just heard that she has been shot by an Afghan soldier – for reasons that are unclear, since her reputation for amiability was unblemished – and that her puppy was sold in the market as a fighting-dog.

It is a story that brings home how lucky we are to live in a benign canine culture. But last week's report on dog-breeding from Professor Sir Patrick Bateson, a Cambridge zoologist, was a sobering reminder that we, too, tolerate a casual cruelty towards these animals that give us so much pleasure.

Professor Bateson's inquiry was commissioned by the Kennel Club after a television documentary that presented harrowing evidence about the impact of pedigree breeding. The distressing images of Cavalier King Charles Spaniels in fitting spasms, because their skulls were too small for their brains, will remain with me for ever.

Sir Patrick has written up his findings with luminous clarity, and I would recommend the report to any dog-owner: you will discover, for example, that humans have been taking pleasure in the company of dogs for at least sixteen thousand years. But Sir Patrick is a scientist, and not a philosopher: he left some uncomfortable ethical questions unanswered.

Kudu has taken to producing a growl when the wonderful dog-walker who looks after him during busy days clips on his lead. It is a duty growl, really, as if he feels obliged to protest about leaving his house with someone other than his owners. When I witnessed it on Tuesday, I apologized to the dog-walker. 'He is,' she demurred, 'the least aggressive dog I have ever known. You should breed from him. He is very handsome.'

Breeding from Kudu so that his kindness is passed down to future generations seems a good thing to do. Breeding from him for the sake of perpetuating that good-looking profile seems frivolous and wrong. But is there, in ethical terms, any difference between the two? And what separates either of these things from the breeder who wants his Cavalier King Charles to have a small head to win prizes?

The simple answer is to distinguish between dogs bred for a practical purpose, and those bred for show.

Kudu is designed for rough shooting. Springers are so-named not because of their Zebedee-like enthusiasm for life, but because they 'spring' birds, putting them up for the guns by snouting around in the bushes. If you want a dog to herd sheep (Collies, for example) or retrieve game (Labradors, and Kudu if he does not get distracted by intriguing smells *en passant*), or to hunt beasts that lurk in burrows (Dachshunds), you need it to be healthy, so genetic engineering in these breeds is likely to promote traits that are in the interests of dog welfare.

If, on the other hand, you want a dog simply as a fashion accessory, you will encourage breeding practices that are almost certainly damaging to your dog's welfare. 'It seems scarcely credible,' Sir Patrick writes, 'that one of the tiny toy breeds, weighing two kilos or less and fitting inside a woman's handbag, could be derived from a wolf.'

Sir Patrick is very tactful, and his affection for dogs is transparent. But the logic of what he says is that toy dogs are as much of an abomination as fighting-dogs and (gulp) should be controlled like Pit Bulls. Oh dear. Such complexities are a world away from the simple moral universe of that Afghan soldier who killed Sandy just because he wanted to.

Why dogs are streets ahead of their owners
6 February 2010

There is nothing more humiliating than a public display of doggy disobedience.

When Kudu is launched from a car directly into a green space he is as biddable as can be: no matter how far he roams, he always returns if called. But when he is walked along a street he is an incorrigible puller on the lead. I can just about hold him, but younger, lighter family members almost hit take-off speed as they are dragged in his wake.

I first put down this panting eagerness to the attractions of the scruffy square of grass where he takes his afternoon turn – it is a gritty, urban dog haven, and the daily offering of olfactory messages is no doubt varied and enticing. But I am now convinced there is a more complicated dynamic at work: these outings are a test of which of us is in charge.

I am training him into road-sense (essential for a city dog), so on the return journey I leave him off the lead and try to walk him to heel. Fat chance. Not once have I persuaded him to walk behind me. He will, if I repeat, 'Stay with me,' in increasingly growly tones, keep to the pavement, and he has got the point about junctions, but he always stays just ahead. He gently pushes up the speed: once I caught myself trotting to keep up, and I am sure he smirked. It is a ritual game of Grandmother's Footsteps, which I can never win, and, after spotting two of my neighbours shaking with laughter by the roadside, I realized it is also a source of local merriment.

We think dogs belong to us, but current theories about the domestication of wolves (from which the modern dog developed) suggest they may have inherited a rather different understanding. One proposition holds that at the end of the Ice Age, when wolves and humans were competing for the same food, alliances of convenience were formed between them: the women and children of hunting communities nurtured animals who would stay near them. Another theory is that clever (and lazy) wolves worked out they could feed themselves without the bother of hunting if they scavenged around human settlements. Both theories suggest a degree of equality, with the decision to collaborate being made as much by the wolf as by the human.

Juliet Clutton-Brock, the distinguished archaeo-zoologist, argues that Late Ice Age humans formed alliances with all sorts of animals; the alliance with wolves endured because we live in similar social structures. 'As with human communities,' she writes, 'the social structure of the wolf is based on a hierarchy of dominant and submissive individuals who are constantly aware of their status in respect to each other.' Other species that might seem wolf-like never developed into dogs because they socialized in a different way.

Thus among African Hunting Dogs (*Lycaon pictus*), 'Social behaviour is more dependent on the mutual regurgitation of food and less on communication by facial expression . . . So that if a man is not prepared to take the regurgitated offerings of a hunting dog into his own mouth his powers of communication with the dog are going to be limited.' On balance I think we should be grateful that these no doubt charming animals took an evolutionary path that did not lead them to the domestic hearth.

All this history is, I am sure, churning atavistically at the back of Kudu's brain as he pulls me along the pavement. Quite why his usual submissiveness should turn to dominance at this particular moment of his day and at no other remains a mystery, but in the course of my researches I encountered an aphoristic reminder that some aspects of dogginess will always remain closed to us: 'Outside of a dog, a book is man's best friend. Inside of a dog, it's too dark to read.' It is attributed to Groucho Marx.

Off on a ski holiday? Be sure to take the dog
19 February 2010

How does a dog come to terms with the chemistry of snow?

The question was prompted by the owner of one of Kudu's smarter Clapham friends, a boisterous young Springer called Tigger. We were discussing the annual skiing holiday, and she described Tigger's attempts to retrieve snowballs; the way a snowball disappears into snow when it lands must be deeply puzzling to an animal bred to retrieve solid objects like dead pheasants, and Tigger, dutiful dog that he is, digs deep before admitting defeat.

But he loves the skiing holiday, I was told, chasing his owners up in the lifts and careening down the slopes after them. My companion did admit that taking a dog skiing is easier if you have your own chalet.

This is the season when, as thoughts turn south to Alpine sun, the owners of privileged dogs agonize about dog care. Most of the time Kudu's friends enjoy a cheerful equality: the pleasures of park and common are open to all. But their lifestyles when the owners are away vary hugely: here lies the great divide between rich dogs and poor dogs.

The distinguished historian Leandra de Lisle tells me she treats the boarding arrangements for her dog as seriously as those she used to make for her children. She booked Fitz (a large Lab) into a local farm, and was interviewed housemaster-style by the owners: 'As they worked through the questions,' she says, 'I found myself giving the kind of answers I would have despised had I heard them from anyone else.' Asked whether Fitz barked or whined, she replied, 'No, but he does talk a lot. He is very intelligent and communicative' – meaning that he does indeed bark and whine, just in varying tones. When Fitz was returned to her the canny dog-hoteliers told her that he had behaved impeccably: 'My sons never had such a good report – I burned with pride.'

In the United States dog-hotels really are like human hotels. At a dinner my wife found herself next to an American businesswoman who described in some detail the facilities then being enjoyed back home by her Schnauzer ('my baby'). Each room in his dog-hotel was equipped with bed, miniature sofa, television set and a selection of DVDs. Kudu quite often watches television by mistake (by sitting on the remote control) but I do not think he enjoys it very much, and for some reason he always seems to pick a shopping channel. I cannot help wondering whether the Schnauzer's system offered those 'adult' channels that all hotels now seem determined their guests should enjoy.

Dog-carers compete fiercely for this top-end business. A former BBC manager of my acquaintance has acquired one offering daily emails with up-to-the-minute news of her Labrador: 'Fudge had a good walk today. I had him out a little longer just because he was having a great time. He really is getting fit, usually by the time we get to the common he just lies in the grass but now he gets involved in the other dogs' games and loves exploring . . .' It takes real literary talent to churn this stuff out day after day, but it is a brilliant business idea: this is just what you want on your BlackBerry to take the edge off any guilt you might feel about leaving Fudge behind while you cane the *piste* in Courchevel.

But what of the dogs at the other end of the economic spectrum? Walking through one of the underpasses by Waterloo Station, I spotted a homeless man asleep with his Alsatian. The man looked sad, sick and scruffy; the dog, curled up against his body, looked sleek and completely contented. Dogs do not really appreciate DVDs in smartly appointed hotel rooms – to be happy, they just need to be with us.

So if you have got the money, buy the chalet, and take him skiing too.

5

In Defence of Dogs

I AWOKE ONE MORNING to find my wife looking at me in a most alarming manner – alarming and, indeed, alarmed: it was almost as if she had found a stranger next to her in bed. 'Did you sleep well?' I enquired, in a tentative manner.

'Actually, no,' came the reply. 'You were talking in your sleep . . . well, not so much talking. You were growling . . . and then you made little woofing noises.'

I have always taken specialist journalism very seriously. When I was appointed Washington correspondent for *Channel 4 News* I went straight out and bought a shelf-load of books about American foreign policy and constitutional theory. When I moved to Paris for the BBC I dutifully ploughed through biographies of François Mitterrand, who was then president. Taking on the diplomatic job at ITN, I did deep background by swotting up on Talleyrand. Being a dog specialist is, in its way, every bit as absorbing as any other discipline: I now have dozens of serious factual books with titles like *If Dogs Could Talk: Exploring the canine mind*, and lots of novels with the word 'dog' in the title – Alexander McCall Smith's *The Dog Who Came In From the Cold* and Kate Atkinson's *Started Early, Took My Dog* are two recent titles that immediately found their way on to our bookshelves.

And if the unsettling incident of doggy sleep-talking is anything to go by, I can be every bit as obsessive and Ancient Marinerish about dogs as I once was about Famous Filibusters in the United States Senate or the importance of the *acquis communautaire* in EU accession negotiations.

The Dog has a way of looking at me that makes me examine my conscience, and honesty compels me to admit that part of the pleasure of being a specialist in a subject is knowing more than other people do – and showing off about it. When it is your professional duty to flaunt your expertise on a regular basis, it of course makes the fun easier to enjoy. And most specialist journalism is a blokeish, nerdy thing – like stamp-collecting or re-building vintage cars. It is probably no accident that I keep my dog library in that most blokeish of environments: my garden shed. I have done most of my dog writing there too.

But it is also true that if you are trying to keep abreast of everything that is written in your field you are bound to spot the odd book or article that deserves to be noticed more widely. The book that forms the basis of this next column is an example.

A dog can sense if it's in bad odour with you
20 March 2010

The BBC has provided me with a piece of kit that allows me to broadcast in studio quality from our basement. It is invaluable for programmes at anti-social hours, when I would rather not schlep across town to a studio. Last Friday, I was pulled off the subs bench to present *Any Questions*, and in the morning I nipped downstairs to read the regular live trail just before the 7.30 a.m. news summary.

Kudu was in the kitchen, happily bashing my stepdaughter with his paw in the hope of being scratched. When I boomed from the radio he leapt to attention, nose a-quiver, clearly discomforted by my disembodied voice.

Why so, when he has often heard me broad-casting in the past? I assume that if I have left the house, he tunes out of our relationship, and does not register that the voice on the radio is mine, whereas on this occasion he knew that I was still about the place. But I cannot know this with any certainty.

An American animal behaviourist, Alexandra

Horowitz, has published a book to help those of us frustrated by the challenge of the canine mind. *Inside of a Dog – What Dogs See, Smell and Know* is based on a proposition from a certain Jacob von Uexküll, an early-twentieth-century German biologist: that to understand the way animals think, we must combine empirical scientific experiments with an imaginative effort to understand their *Umwelt*, or 'self-world'.

Dr Horowitz is prepared to go to considerable lengths to think herself into a dog's *Umwelt*. She recommends 'spending an afternoon at the height of a dog' where 'the world is full of long skirts and trouser legs dancing with every footfall of their wearer', and the environment 'is a more odoriferous one, for smells loiter and fester in the ground'. I suspect she would disapprove of those owners now prettifying their dogs for next week's Crufts. She argues that when we stick dogs in a bath, we deprive them of an important part of their identity: 'The mildest fragrance that cleansers come in is still an olfactory insult to a dog.'

I first encountered Dr Horowitz when I interviewed her last year about an experiment into whether dogs really can distinguish between good and bad behaviour. She left the dogs alone in a room with a titbit that their owners had expressly forbidden them to eat. Some ate the titbit; the owner was told, and the dog was ticked off. On other occasions, the researchers removed it before the dog could eat it, yet still told the owner that their pet had been disobedient, provoking the predictable ticking-off.

How did the dogs behave? The innocents who had been deprived of the titbits were just as likely to look guilty (lowered eyes, slump in the gait, faint wagging of the tail) as those who had sinned. In other words, the dogs were simply reacting to their owners' behaviour, and the guilty look had nothing to do with what they had or had not done.

Kudu is good at holding eye contact, and when he gazes at one of us in a soulful way, it feels very much as if he is trying to communicate. After studying Dr Horowitz's book, I am persuaded that he is in fact 'reading' us, working out how we expect him to behave so that he can use this to his advantage. And I suspect the reaction to my radio broadcast reflected his shock at behaviour he could not understand. If Dr Horowitz is right, dogs really do know us very well indeed. She writes eloquently about the information they gather by sniffing; they can tell whether you are afraid, whether you have cancer and 'if you have had sex, smoked a cigarette (or done both of these things in succession), just had a snack, or just run a mile'. Most unsettling – but it is a very good book.

Here is another confession: I enjoy feeling indignant.

This is a late-flowering pleasure, as for most of my professional life I have had to keep such emotions firmly in check for the sake of the impartiality that is quite rightly expected from broadcasters. There are two sides to most stories, and I am so used to reporting both that I sometimes worry I might lose the ability to hold an opinion of my own.

Kudu has taught me that on the subject of dogs I do in fact have very strong views indeed, and, I suspect like most dog-owners, I suffer regular episodes of dog-rage when faced with the petty restrictions that modern life imposes on canine freedom. Why do taxi drivers look at you with such horror when your perfectly clean animal jumps into the back and sits placidly on the floor? Why are dogs banned from post offices, which do not sell any food and make their customers queue for so long that any dog left tied up outside might reasonably assume it had been abandoned? Why do some people press themselves against railings and shop fronts with comedy expressions of terror on their faces when you walk along the pavement with your perfectly friendly hound on a lead?

It is dogism, pure and simple.

Beware: dogism is sweeping the land
20 March 2010

Urban dog that he is, Kudu has developed reasonably good manners for dealing with other users of public spaces: he gives a polite sniff to members of his own species he encounters in parks or on commons, but never approaches a human without being invited (in the early days he did, it is true, once or twice use a trouser-leg as a lamppost, but he seems to have got over that).

Last weekend, while being walked by my wife, he scampered – nose down in the eternal quest for the next smell – within a couple of yards of two children playing on Clapham Common. It was a couple of yards too close for the liking of their father, who began abusing Kudu and tried quite hard to kick him. I have written before about cultures that are less dog-friendly than our own, and this man clearly came from one. He pursued my wife across the common, wagging an admonitory finger and berating 'You English' for keeping 'killer dogs', all of which, he shouted, should be killed themselves.

I blame the politicians. All the killer-dog talk from people who should know better has stirred up an ugly mood, and dogism is sweeping the country. Even our local borough newspaper, *Lambeth Life*, has jumped on the bandwagon: 'Dogs collared in new policy' is the splash headline in this week's edition, and there is a terrifying photograph of a snarling brute being held at bay at the end of two steel poles.

The scapegoating of dogs can lead to some ugly places. The Roman habit of crucifying a dog annually is notorious – the city's dogs were blamed for failing to raise the alarm when the Capitol was attacked by Gauls in 390 BC. Less well known are the show trials that were conducted against dogs and other animals from the Middle Ages right up until the beginning of the last century.

Many of the more curious cases in the seminal work *The Criminal Prosecution and Capital Punishment of Animals* involve other species. Grasshoppers were tried in Lombardy in 1452, snails at Macon in 1487, and there was a long case brought against weevils by the wine-growers of St Julien in 1587. But a show trial of a dog called Porter near Chichester was recorded as late as 1771, and in 1906 in Switzerland a dog went on trial with two men (his owner and the owner's son) for robbery and murder. The men got life, but the dog was held to have been the ringleader and was executed.

The law is not quite sure what to make of dogs. Formally they are treated 'like other personal and movable chattels' and that, of course, makes nonsense of putting them on trial. But because we anthropomorphize them there is a tugging temptation for lawyers to treat them like humans.

Last week I talked to a couple of top family lawyers about a newspaper story that couples are drawing up 'pre-pups' to avoid a row over the dog should they divorce. I couldn't get the story to stand up, but a leading QC mused, 'I have often wondered whether any such dispute should be resolved by pure property law, or whether there is room for application of the principles arising under the Children Act – the first and paramount consideration is the best interest of the child (or dog?)?'

This could open up dangerous territory. Courts work on the premise that the best interests of a child in a divorce are usually served by giving custody to the mother; would they be willing to make a similar presumption, perhaps in favour of the man of the house, where a dog is concerned? I was once stopped on my bike outside the butcher by a fan of these columns who wanted to tell me that he recognized many of his own dog's foibles in my Kudu stories. He waxed lyrical – at some length – about the fun the two of them had on their walks, and then his face fell. 'Until, that is, the divorce,' he said. 'My ex-wife took him when we broke up . . .' The poor chap was clearly much more upset about losing his dog than he was about the collapse of his marriage, and (without, of course, knowing the other side of the story) I could not help feeling he would have been a very good master.

The straightforward 'dogs are property' approach at least keeps responsibility for their behaviour firmly focused on the owners. Identifying killer breeds has always seemed flawed to me: I think you can make pretty much any dog into a killer if you try, and even the most terrifying breeds can be brought up nicely.

The problem with that theory is that Kudu proves it isn't true. I have concluded that absolutely nothing could persuade him into aggression: his only response to trouble is lying on his back and offering you an eyeful of tummy and testicles.

When the fate of a dog tore a nation in two
3 April 2010

Battersea Park was a frenzy of spring mulching, mowing and planting. Siren invitations to linger at the café were being fired from the Chelsea yummy mummies, and Kudu received an indecent proposal from a gardener: his Springer bitch, the man politely explained, had been let down by a suitor at the last moment, and would Kudu care to pop round for the afternoon? He offered 'a hundred quid or the pick of the litter'. It seemed a somewhat casual way for Kudu to take on the responsibilities of fatherhood, and I declined on his behalf.

We sought refuge in the park's quieter walks and, hidden away near the river, I found the Brown Dog Memorial. It is a life-size bronze of a terrier with an expressively cocked head and alert ears. A sentimental piece, but it carries a shocking inscription: 'In memory of the Brown Terrier Dog done to Death in the Laboratories of University College in February 1903, after having endured Vivisection extending over more than two months and having been handed from one Vivisector to another till death came to its Release . . . Men and Women of England, how long shall these things be?'

The Brown Dog Affair was one of the great political controversies of the day.

Public vivisection was – extraordinary though it may seem – a common, if highly controversial, practice in late Victorian and Edwardian Britain. In 1902 the mongrel that came to be known as the Brown Dog was cut open before an audience of medical students by Professor Ernest Starling of University College (a scientist of real stature). The dog survived for another two months before Starling opened him up again, inspected the previous surgery, and then passed him on to two other scientists. They administered half an hour of electric shocks before the dog was killed.

The lecture had been infiltrated by two Swedish animal-rights activists, and they published a harrowing account – claiming the dog had not been anaesthetized and showed 'the signs of intense suffering'. There was this gem of invective: 'The lecturer, attired in the bloodstained surplice of the priest of vivisection, has tucked up his sleeves and is now comfortably smoking a pipe, whilst, with hands coloured crimson, he arranges the electrical circuit for the stimulation that will follow. Now and then, he makes a funny remark, which is appreciated by those around him.'

One of the scientists involved sued – and won. The World League Against Vivisection responded with a public subscription for a statue to commemorate the dog 'done to death' in the name of science – not the rather cute number in Battersea Park today but a great granite and bronze monument, standing seven foot six tall. It was erected at the Latchmere Estate, a housing project for the poor just opened by Battersea Council.

Battersea was most definitely not a place for the Chelsea yummy mummies in those days: it was full of slums and a hotbed of radicalism. But medical students from University College sent raiding parties over the river armed with crowbars to destroy the statue. They were repeatedly beaten back by the Battersea workers. An extraordinary coalition rallied to the Brown Dog cause – suffragettes, Sinn Fein activists, trade unionists and radical Liberals.

Defending the statue became a symbol for radical causes in general. The 'anti-doggers' responded with riots in Trafalgar Square – on one occasion mounted police fought running battles with more than a thousand students.

Eventually – in March 1910 – Battersea Council gave in: the statue was quietly removed in a pre-dawn operation under the protection of 120 police officers. The new statue in the park, by the sculptor Nicola Hicks, was made in 1985.

Kudu became impatient when I lingered in front of it – pondering this remarkable and largely forgotten history. He scarcely gave it a sniff – in fact he did not even bother to pee on the plinth.

At about the time of the Brown Dog riots, French society was being torn apart by the traumatic saga of Captain Alfred Dreyfus, the young Jewish artillery officer who was falsely accused of treason and sentenced to hard labour on Devil's Island. The Dreyfus Affair raised painful questions about French and Jewish identity, inspired Zionism and thus led eventually to the foundation of Israel. It says something about this country that while all of that was going on across the Channel we were worrying about a dog. The Brown Dog Affair opens an intriguing window on to Edwardian Britain: it became a focus for all sorts of political and social currents that were swirling through the early years of the last century.

The list of *dramatis personae* is impressive in itself. Ernest

Starling, the University College professor who led the vivi-section of the Brown Dog, was the man who discovered hormones – largely through his vivisection experiments. In the libel case that inspired the Brown Dog statue, the pro-dog lawyer – whose diatribes against canine mistreatment make my own episodes of dog-rage look positively insipid – was Stephen Coleridge, a son of the former Chief Justice Lord Coleridge (and great-great-nephew of the poet), who went on to help found the NSPCC. George Bernard Shaw turned up to see the statue unveiled and John Archer, a Battersea councillor who championed its preservation, was Britain's first elected official of African descent.

Anyone worried about the way modern students behave would do well to read the accounts of what was apparently considered normal student protest at the time: the Brown Dog Riots were exactly that, riots, not peaceful demonstrations that went wrong. The students wore dog masks (one Cambridge undergraduate who joined in was arrested for 'barking like a dog') and chanted this piece of 'doggerel' (forgive me – an irresistible pun):

> As we go walking after dark,
> We turn our steps to Latchmere Park
> And there we see, to our surprise,
> A little brown dog that stands and lies
> Ha ha ha, he he he,
> Little brown dog how we hate thee.

On the day the riots reached a climax, 10 December 1907, the students fought the police for several hours. When they were eventually driven off the streets a local doctor told a newspaper that their failure to hold out for longer reflected the 'utter degeneration' of the youth of the day – which suggests their cause had support from a class of person who should have known better.

That may reflect a reaction against the way the Brown Dog cause became – rather weirdly – identified with the suffragette movement. The late actress and academic Coral Lansbury, who wrote a rich account of the affair and the cultural forces behind it, argued that 'Women were the most fervent supporters of anti-vivisection, not simply for reasons of humanity, but because the vivisected animal stood for the vivisected woman: the woman strapped to the gynaecologist's table; the woman strapped and bound in the pornographic fiction of the period.' Warming to her theme later in the book, she writes that 'Woman's suffrage had very little in common with anti-vivisection, but the two become confusedly entwined through the accident of circumstance: the image of the vivisected dog blurred and became one with the militant suffragette being force-fed in Brixton Prison.'

Coral Lansbury admits (boasts?) that 'many people will be puzzled and disturbed' by her book, and I am never quite sure whether it makes sense to impose the language of late-twentieth-century radical academic discourse on the past, but it is certainly true that many suffragettes were prominent pro-doggers. Opponents of women's suffrage recognized the connection between the two protest movements by making barking noises when they disrupted suffragette meetings.

It is also striking that the Brown Dog was one of the few causes that succeeded in uniting what we might broadly call 'the forces of the Left' of the early twentieth century; the socialist culture of a working-class area like Battersea was very male, and its leaders were not especially well disposed towards brainy middle-class women living in Chelsea across the river (Sylvia Pankhurst has a blue plaque in Cheyne Row, just up from Battersea Bridge). But both groups were moved by the Brown Dog's story, and both saw their enemy in the bullying yahoos from the medical profession, who seemed to represent all that was worst about the moneyed male Establishment. One modern writer has argued that the Brown Dog's mongrel nature was a reflection of the political coalition he inspired.

Of the Brown Dog's character, we of course know nothing at all; he is, as it were, all symbol, a universal Platonic Idea of Dog rather than an individual creature you can imagine thumping its tail when you open the front door. And in the voluminous literature this dog has generated there is a tendency to give him qualities that reflect political agendas. One radical writer has, for example, criticized the modern statue that inspired my column on the grounds that it is too twee and 'heritage', and not as defiant as the original.

I find the Brown Dog a much richer and more intriguing subject than the tale of another dog commemorated by public monument – Greyfriars Bobby. We know much more about

Bobby's character than we do about the Brown Dog's, and he seems pretty bonkers to me.

Bobby's story is well known. A Skye Terrier, he belonged to a certain John Gray, who worked as a constable and night-watchman for the Edinburgh police. Gray died of tuberculosis in 1858, just two years after acquiring Bobby, and was buried in Greyfriars churchyard. For the next fourteen years, until his own death in 1872, Bobby watched over his master's grave. He was nearly destroyed as a feral dog in 1867, but the Lord Provost of Edinburgh personally paid his dog-licence and gave him a collar. When he died Angela Burdett Coutts (the immensely rich Victorian philanthropist who, in a twist that brings together the Brown Dog and Greyfriars Bobby stories, was very much involved in establishing the NSPCC alongside the lawyer Stephen Coleridge) commissioned a statue to stand at the end of the George IV Bridge in his memory.

I find Bobby's story shockingly sad. There is a narrow line dividing doggy fidelity and canine monomania, and Bobby had definitely crossed it. I have met one or two Labradors who have become monomaniac in their devotion to tennis balls: they show almost no interest in anything but fetching and will continue to offer you a ball to throw for as long as you are prepared to do it. Bobby's fixation with his master's grave was a similarly unhealthy narrowing of his life's focus.

But he has, of course, been widely celebrated as a model of fidelity, and his story has inspired books and films. The most famous of them is Eleanor Atkinson's sentimental novel *Greyfriars Bobby*, first published in 1912 and reincarnated as a Disney film in 1961. Ms Atkinson was born in the American Midwest and never visited Edinburgh, but that did not stop her giving her imagination full rein when it came to evoking 'Scottishness': John Gray, Bobby's master, becomes 'Auld Jock', and some of Atkinson's renditions of the local dialect are completely impenetrable. Here is the graveyard caretaker, Mr Brown, explaining why he enjoys Bobby's visits to his sickbed: 'Ilka morn he fetches 'is bane up, thinkin' it a braw giftie for an ill man. An' syne he veesits me twa times i' the day, juist bidin' a wee on the hearthstane, lollin' 'is tongue an' waggin' 'is tail, cheerfu' like. Bobby has mair gude sense in 'is heid than mony a man wha comes ben the house, wi lang face, to let me ken I'm gangin to dee.' No? Me neither. But the book is considered a classic.

Of course, the really bonkers behaviour is not Bobby's, it is that of his fans. There is now a red granite headstone erected in his memory, and people put sticks there for him to chase.

6

Mad Dogs, Hero Dogs
and Your Health

I hope happiness hasn't gone to the dogs
17 April 2010

KUDU DID A SPELL at boarding school while we spent a weekend in Scotland. His best friend, the boisterous Poodle, Teddy, was there too, and I know he felt at home because the headmistress told me he tried to climb on to her bed.

But his behaviour on his return suggested he had been delivered from the fires of hell. Whimpering with excitement, he found as many of his toys as he could and delivered them as sacrificial offerings. He made victory circuits of the garden, sprinted from the top of the house to the bottom of the basement stairs, and licked the cats until they dripped with slobber. It was only three days, for goodness' sake!

It had been a brainy weekend. Our host, an art historian, was working on the definitive history of English collecting, and one of the other guests was editing a magazine supplement on the Far East. My wife held her own with her heavyweight television documentaries, but these were deep waters for a dog columnist. So I threw a question into the conversational pot that I felt had a bit of intellectual heft: why are dogs – black ones especially – associated with depression?

Churchill made the phrase 'black dog' famous. John Colville, his private secretary, traced it to the nursery. He reported that the great man's doctor would sometimes call after breakfast: 'Churchill, not especially pleased to see any visitor at such an hour, might excuse a certain early-morning surliness by saying, "I have got a black dog on my back today." That was an expression much used by old-fashioned English nannies.'

Much academic energy has been poured into the search for the origins of the phrase, and most theories lead back to Dr Johnson, who used it just as Churchill did. 'The black dog I hope always to resist,' he wrote. 'When I rise my breakfast is solitary, the black dog wakes to share it, from breakfast to dinner he continues barking . . .'

But all this etymology rather misses the point. A good-natured dog like Kudu inspires cheerfulness, not misery, and he usually lifts me out of low spirits rather than the reverse, so why did the association with depression arise in the first place?

It is true that dogs do not have a well-developed sense of humour. I have been reading a book of dog stories from the *Spectator* of the 1880s and 1890s. There are plenty of anecdotes about the canine ability to find home (including one, which I do not quite believe, about a dog that worked its way back to a farm near Gloucester from 'the interior of Canada'), and there is a good story about a church-going dog that felt the vicar's sermon was too long and took the collection plate round in its mouth to shut him up. But the offerings under 'Dogs' Sense of Humour' are decidedly thin. One correspondent records a dog watching a man with a serious limp struggling down some stairs: 'When the invalid was nearly at the foot of the stairs the dog began to follow, limping on three legs in humorous imitation of our poor afflicted friend . . .' Hmm.

But the fact that dogs are not great wits does not mean they make you want to slit your wrists.

The clue to the conundrum was provided by our scholarly weekend host, who pointed me towards a book called *Saturn and Melancholy*, written by three German academics in the 1930s. To explain why dogs are associated with melancholia, they quote an early-sixteenth-century German translation of a fifth-century Greek treatise (stay with me) on Egyptian hieroglyphics, which states that 'The dog, more gifted and sensitive than other beasts, has a very serious nature and can fall victim to madness, and like deep thinkers is inclined to be always on the hunt, smelling things out . . .' And there is this in the seventeenth-century English work *The Anatomy of Melancholy*: 'Of all other animals, dogs are most subject to this malady. I could relate many stories of dogs that have dyed of grief, and pined away for loss of their masters . . .'

So it is not that dogs make us depressed, it is the fact that they get depressed themselves that has given rise to the association. And here is a terrible thought that flows in consequence: perhaps those doe-eyes that Kudu gives me when I leave him are not put on for show – perhaps, indeed, the absurd pantomime when we were reunited after our weekend apart represented genuine relief. Is it possible that when we are away he is, like a 'deep thinker', a prey to dark existential uncertainties?

My wife recently took him to visit her sister, and left him in the house while the two of them went out for a couple of hours. On her return he leapt into the car and refused all inducements to come out – even when offered the chance to chase a fox. If I allow myself to think that each time he is left alone he really does wonder whether we shall ever return, I may stop going out altogether.

This column proved prophetic: a few months after it appeared, a team at Bristol University published a paper which suggested that some dogs do indeed think they have been permanently abandoned every time their owners leave the house. Quite a lot of dogs, in fact, apparently think this way, and that is why so many owners come home to find lumps of upholstery scattered all over the floor: 'About half the dogs in Britain may at some point perform separation-related behaviours, barking and destroying objects around the house, when they are apart from their owners,' said Professor Mike Mendel, of the university's animal welfare department, who led the research team.

Working with a group of twenty-four rescue dogs, the researchers trained them to know that when a bowl was placed in a certain position it would contain food, and that when it was placed at another location it would be empty. They then moved the bowl to a position somewhere between the 'positive' and 'negative' locations. Those dogs which 'ran fast to these ambiguous locations as if expecting the positive food reward' were classed as optimists; those that did not were classed as pessimists – and these were the dogs most likely to exhibit extreme forms of separation anxiety.

I worry about what experiments of this kind do to the mental equilibrium of the dogs involved. More than anything else, dogs need to be able to trust their owners – there is an especially terrible example of the breaking of this bond in the Hardy poem I quote on page 133. The dogs in the Bristol experiment had to learn to accept what must have seemed a somewhat eccentric feeding routine from their human handlers – only to find it broken in an apparently capricious way. That must surely be enough to make any dog – especially one from a re-homing centre – wonder about the Meaning of Life.

Kudu has, mercifully, never been a great chewer: if we leave the bedroom door open when we are out, he collects a small pile of our clothes into the centre of the bed and sleeps on them, but he has never taken revenge for our absences by destroying the furniture.

His suitcase obsession has, however, become pathological. When my wife and I were preparing for a rare weekend away together, his reaction to our packing was so extreme that we felt guilty all the way to the airport. He cried – I mean really cried, so that his cheeks were wet with tears. He then climbed into the suitcase and refused to move until sternly spoken to.

But I take this as a reassuring indication of his intelligence, and therefore of his ability to distinguish between the likely duration of separations. If he knows that a packed suitcase means a member of the household will be away for several days, he presumably also knows that watching me potter off on my bicycle means something less dramatic.

I also wonder whether the suitcase thing is related to my daughter's departure to live in her own flat. She is only a few streets away, and she often pops back to see him, but the firmly shut door of what used to be Eleanor's bedroom is a reminder of the terrible fact that all dogs must confront at some stage: people do sometimes leave. While Kudu was boarding with his dog-walker for a long weekend Eleanor took him down to the Sussex coast for a day by the sea; the dog-walker reported that after Eleanor dropped him back he lay by the door whimpering for hours.

The most extreme example of separation anxiety I have found is the account given by the German zoologist and animal behaviourist Konrad Lorenz of his relationship with his Alsatian/Chow cross – it is so extreme that, were it not for his eminent reputation as a Nobel Prize-winning scientist, I would suspect him of telling porkies.

Stasi was born in his house in 1940 (this was obviously before the foundation of the German Democratic Republic, so I assume there was no sinister connection between her name and the notorious East German secret police) and quickly responded to training. In his book *Man Meets Dog*, Lorenz writes, 'She learnt the rudiments of canine education, walking on the lead, walking to heel, "lying down", astonishingly quickly. She was more or less spontaneously house-clean and safe with poultry . . .'

In September that year Lorenz had to leave home to take up a university post at Königsberg, and on returning for Christmas he got the sort of frenzied welcome that is one of the universal pleasures of dog-ownership. But when he prepared to leave again things took a distressing turn: 'When the trunks were packed and my departure became imminent, the misery of poor Stasi waxed to the point of desperation, almost to a neurosis. She would not eat and her breathing became abnormal, very shallow and punctuated now and then by deep sighs.' Stasi followed him to the station and made her last desperate attempt to stay at her master's side as the train pulled away: 'She suddenly shot forward, rushing alongside the train, and leaping on to it, three carriages in front of the one on which I was standing in order to prevent her jumping on to it.' Lorenz caught her scruff and tipped her off.

Stasi returned home but underwent a profound change in her personality. She began killing chickens and fouling the house, became disobedient and aggressive, and committed a long list of crimes, including 'the burglary of a rabbit hutch, with much ensuing bloodshed, and finally the tearing of the postman's trousers'. Eventually she had to be expelled from the house and was kept locked in the back yard.

Lorenz's description of what happened when he came home for the summer holidays is a *tour de force*. At first Stasi did not recognize him, and when he approached the area where she was confined she rushed ferociously in his direction. Then she caught his scent on the wind:

What now took place I shall never forget. In the midst of a heated onrush, she stopped abruptly and stiffened into a statue. Her mane was still ruffled, her tail down and her ears flat, but her nostrils were wide, wide open, inhaling greedily the message carried on the wind. Now the raised crest subsided, a shiver ran through her body and she pricked up her ears. I had expected her to throw herself at me in a burst of joy, but she did not. The mental suffering which had been so severe as to alter the dog's whole personality, causing this most tractable of creatures to forget manners, laws and order for months, could not fade into nothingness in a second. Her hind legs gave way, her nose was directed skywards, something happened in her throat, and then the mental torture of months found outlet in the hair-raising yet beautiful tones of a wolf's howl. For a long time, perhaps half a minute, she howled, then, like a thunderbolt, she was upon me. I was enveloped in a whirlwind of ecstatic canine joy . . .

Now that is what I call real dog writing! The passage ends with the two of them taking happy summer swims in the Danube.

The Bristol experiment prompted a leader in the *Guardian*, which argued that some dogs 'feel hounded' (ho ho) because of what the paper called 'a dismissive language of analogy' – by which it meant expressions like 'dog-eared', 'dog-tired' and 'sick as a dog'. The leader writer was clearly not a dog-lover: to me the negative connotations of all those expressions are mitigated by the dog-tag. When a book is dog-eared it is not just scruffy and torn – it is well-worn through being much handled with affection, like an old family pet which has dutifully put up with years of friendly rough-and-tumble from the children. To be dog-tired evokes Kudu after a good country ramble: if he is really exhausted he can pass from hyperactive hedgerow-sniffing mode into total oblivion by the fireside within seconds; this is exactly the condition of glowing physical collapse I so much enjoy after a good day's skiing, and very different from the troubled, nervous tiredness that comes from working too hard. And while I would obviously rather not be sick as a dog, the phrase is never used to describe a really serious condition – like cancer, for example: to me it suggests over-indulgence at Christmas lunch, the consequence of accepting another slice of Christmas pudding and another glass of port rather than heading out for the sort of bracing walk that might make you dog-tired instead.

Dogs can be both brave and brazen
1 May 2010

Just before I went on air with Radio 4's *Sunday* programme the broadcast assistant (or BA), who has the job of making sure everyone is where they should be at the right moment, told me she had been woken that morning by a nightmare; she had dreamt that I had decided to come to work by tram (the programme is broadcast from Manchester, so this is not entirely fanciful) and arrived late for my own show.

Dreams about live broadcasting are common. When I presented the lunchtime television news I worried much more about getting stuck in the lavatory at the last moment than I did about fluffing my lines. And in my days as a Washington correspondent in the 1980s I had a recurring nightmare that, in the middle of some earnest discussion of Ronald Reagan's latest arms initiative, I would be overwhelmed by an uncontrollable impulse to take my trousers down. But this is the first time anyone has had an anxiety dream on my behalf, and must surely be counted a tribute to the BA's sense of corporate responsibility.

And, lo, on the train home after the programme I found a story about a BBC man who really had missed his slot – because of a dog.

I was reading a 1948 essay on the role of dogs during the Second World War. In the description of their value in guarding VPs (Vulnerable Points), I came across the following illustration of canine efficiency:

Another incident worth repeating was when a V.P. dog was with his handler, patrolling the perimeter of a Broadcasting Station. It was a very sultry evening and an announcer, who had a break in the programme for a few minutes, came out into the night air for relaxation. The dog, however, caught his scent and the handler, after releasing the dog, suddenly heard a scream. On going forward ... he found the announcer half-way up a Pylon with the dog sitting threateningly below. The BBC apologized later for a 'technical hitch'.

My interest in warrior dogs had been aroused when Kudu and I visited the memorial to Animals in War on the central reservation of Park Lane – we had been tempted to Hyde Park for our daily walk by the spring sunshine, and until now I had only really seen the memorial when stuck in heavy traffic.

It definitely '*vaut le détour*'. The experience of war is represented by a sixty-foot wall of Portland stone. A column of animals is making its way through a gap at its centre, and there is a magnificent bronze dog at the head of the column, its bearing suggesting a confident survivor striding into a better future.

But I do wonder about the inscription; 'Animals and War', it reads, and, in smaller lettering, 'They had no choice.' Of course, the horses (eight million of them died in the First World War), mules and dogs who served on the front line had no choice about being sent to war, but neither did most of the humans they fought alongside. They did, however, have a choice about the way they acted – and the fact (also recorded on the memorial) that there is a medal for those animals that show valour recognizes it. You have to make a choice to be brave.

My views about the canine capacity for making moral choices have been heavily influenced by the recent discovery that Kudu is capable of grave moral turpitude. Not generally a greedy beast, he does have a weakness for cat food, and we long ago realized that the cats' bowls had to be kept on a windowsill out of his reach (at least, so we thought).

Usually he goes to bed when we do, but while my wife was away on business recently he took to roaming late around the house . . . and when he did come to bed he smelt suspiciously of fish – like a boozer with telltale breath returning from a bender. An inspection of the cats' bowls confirmed our suspicions – they were cleaned out. And he must know this is wrong, because he never tries it in our presence.

Would he be any good in a war? On my last Afghanistan trip I was shown Springer sniffing skills at Camp Bastion (we were sworn not to reveal the treat the dogs were given when they found explosives, and it is probably the only genuine military secret I have ever been privy to). But I searched the list of mine-detecting dogs used during the Second World War for any mention of his breed in vain.

The explanation lay in the training and selection process: successful applicants had to be 'battle inoculated', and that involved a rigorous regime of tests: all sorts of 'noises off' such as Bren guns, heavy explosions at close range and swooping aircraft had to be inculcated into the training, every sort of distraction was introduced – pinioned rabbits, sheep, game, lumps of meat and even 'in season bitches' were used as deterrents.

The bangs would not have bothered him in the least – he has good gun-dog genes. But when it comes to game and bitches, distraction is his middle name.

After the column above appeared I received a very nice letter from an organization called the Anglican Society for the Welfare of Animals, enclosing a pamphlet by Louise Clark titled *Animals in War*, which records an impressive list of individual acts of canine courage and devotion. At the outbreak of hostilities in 1914 a terrier called Prince managed to find its way from Hammersmith to the French town of Armentières, where it joined its master on the front line. Another star of the trenches was Stubby, a Bull Terrier mix, who woke up sleeping soldiers during a gas attack and bought them vital time to put on their masks, and in the Second World War a Collie known simply as War Dog No. 471/322 became adept at helping commandos in Italy and North Africa by quietly licking them awake when danger threatened. On the home front there was Irma the Blitz Dog: she was trained to sniff out people buried alive beneath rubble and is said to have located more than twenty people, including two small girls, who were dug out after Irma repeatedly returned to an area that rescue workers had already searched. Louise Clark's pamphlet also reports the shocking use of dogs as suicide bombers: 'The worst task befell the dogs in the Russian army,' she writes, 'which used dogs as living explosives to run under tanks carrying a bomb.'

The pamphlet came out in 2010 (the Society that published it was only established in 2000) and the monument to Animals in War, which Kudu and I visited near Hyde Park, was only opened in 2004. Interest in war service as a discreet area of animal welfare seems to be a very modern phenomenon. There is now a charity called Nowzad Dogs, dedicated to looking after strays that have been caught up in the Afghan conflict.

And the way armies use dogs is definitely more appealing than it used to be. Dogs were once primarily employed to fight. Hammurabi, the King of Babylonia (in around 2100 BC), sent his warriors into battle accompanied by huge hounds; Babylonian bas-reliefs of the period portray them as powerful Mastiff-like creatures. The Roman philosopher emperor Marcus Aurelius is shown with dogs clad in armour on his memorial column. And Henry VIII sent hundreds of war dogs to help Charles V of Spain to fight the French – they were reported to have acquitted themselves with great credit at the siege of Valencia.

But in modern warfare dogs have more usually been used as guards, messengers or rescue workers. I particularly enjoy the story of the dogs that went into action with the stretcher-bearers of Airborne Divisions during the Second World War. They came down on their own parachutes and were then ordered to 'quarter the ground much in the same manner that a Spaniel hunts through rough cover', looking for injured para-troopers. So much more suitable for a nicely brought-up dog than ripping people's throats out!

A maudlin dog after reading Hardy
15 May 2010

A dog-walking social life offers plenty of opportunity for variety. Every dog-walking circle has its regular hours: if I go to Battersea Park early I usually meet MPs' wives and the Chelsea set; around nine the park is full of dog-owning parents from the school outside the park gates, and by half past I can be sure of finding my Stockwell neighbours gossiping in the lakeside café.

But south London is plagued by road works, and the Dog and I have had to break with routine, going at all sorts of times to all sorts of places to avoid the traffic. On a late outing to Clapham Common we met Kudu's regular dog-walker exercising her charges.

Kudu sniffed hello to his muckers and I went to investigate the silver bundle she carried in her arms. It was, she thought, a Collie crossed with a German

Shepherd, still too young for its second jab and so not yet able to mix with the other dogs. She had acquired it from a dog-rescue worker who had brought it back from Ireland; discovered by a postman, it had been tethered in a river, left to die there at the age of five weeks.

Wanting an animal to die but lacking the courage to kill it is a uniquely human failing. And it is difficult to understand the mind of someone who can feel enough for a dog to look after it for several weeks, then leave it to face starvation or drowning. Perhaps whoever was responsible eased their conscience with faith in the Providence that guides passing posties.

There is a chilling poem on this subject by Thomas Hardy, called 'The Mongrel'. It tells the story of a man who wants to drown his dog because he cannot pay his tax bill (a slightly unlikely premise, but there we are), so he throws a stick into the sea for the dog to retrieve when he knows the tide will carry it away. As the mongrel battles furiously to stay afloat,

> The loving eyes of the dog inclined
> To the man he held as a god enshrined,
> With no suspicion in his mind
> That this had all been meant.

But at the last moment, as he is drowning, the poor creature realizes he has been had.

> The faith that had shone in that mongrel's eyes
> That his owner would save him by and by
> Turned to much like a curse as he sank to die,
> And a loathing of mankind.

I have always found Hardy a depressing writer: his novels reveal a quite astonishing capacity for imagining the very worst that can happen in any given situation, and the unforgiving Fate, which is such a feature of his books, seems to have afflicted his own non-fictional dog life too. Hardy liked to show people round the graves of his pets when they called at his home; his fellow novelist E. M. Forster remarked on how many of them had died violently (sliced in two under the wheels of a train and so on). 'I don't know how it is . . .' said Hardy, '. . . but of course we have only buried those pets whose bodies were recovered. Many were never seen again.' Forster reported later that he could scarcely keep a straight face because 'it was so like one of Hardy's novels or poems'.

Virginia Woolf, by contrast, becomes an altogether more cheerful writer when she deals with dogs. Just after completing *The Waves* (generally considered her masterpiece, but not the easiest read) she produced a witty biography of Elizabeth Barrett Browning's Spaniel, Flush, which became an instant bestseller. She also wrote about human treachery towards dogs, but with a light touch.

Her short story 'Gipsy, the Mongrel' begins with a farmer who, like the Irish postie, finds a 'little scrap of a dog' tied up in a wicker basket in a snowy hedgerow. The gypsies who abandoned it had left a hunk of bread, 'which shows,' says one of the characters, 'that they hadn't the heart to kill her'. The farmer prepares to drown the dog in a water butt, but just as he is about to do the deed she smiles at him. 'You can't drown a puppy who grins in the face of death,' declares the farmer.

Gipsy the Mongrel survives to live a rackety life of dog crime (killing a favourite cat, giving birth to a bastard puppy under the table during a dinner party, pinching a leg of mutton, etc.) but every time she is threatened with the ultimate punishment she pulls off the grinning trick. Eventually she disappears on another snowy night, answering a mysterious whistle, and leaving the reader wondering whether she ever died at all.

I am not sure whether this is in any way relevant, but Kudu has become a terrible affection addict recently – endlessly resting his head on our knees and bashing us with a paw if we do not stroke him. Perhaps on those nocturnal rambles I mentioned in my last column he has been sneaking Hardy's poems from the bookshelf. I must wean him on to Virginia Woolf instead.

Hardy's near contemporary Rudyard Kipling was famously skilled at writing about animals (witness *The Jungle Book*, *The Just So Stories* and *Thy Servant A Dog*) and he has left us an even sadder dog poem than the one above. Earlier I quoted Jerome K. Jerome's verdict on the foolishness of dogs' love for us – Kipling points to our foolishness in loving them. The first three stanzas of 'The Power of the Dog' will give you the general drift:

> There is sorrow enough in the natural way
> From men and women to fill our day;
> But when we are certain of sorrow in store,
> Why do we always arrange for more?
> *Brothers and sisters, I beg you beware*
> *Of giving your heart to a dog to tear.*
>
> Buy a pup and your money will buy
> Love unflinching that cannot lie –
> Perfect passion and worship fed
> By a kick in the ribs or a pat on the head.
> *Nevertheless it is hardly fair*
> *To risk your heart for a dog to tear.*
>
> When the fourteen years which Nature permits

Are closing in asthma, or tumour, or fits,
And the vet's unspoken prescription runs
To lethal chambers or loaded guns,
Then you'll find – it's your own affair
But . . . you've given your heart to a dog to tear.

If Kudu makes it to twenty – Springers often live rather longer than Kipling's 'fourteen years which nature permits' – I shall have got beyond my allotted three score years and ten before he goes and will be into extra time. So I have not worried too much about his death. But a surprising number of people have said to me that they will not get a dog because they know they will have to watch it die.

Grief for a dead dog is something that can only really be understood by other dog-owners – civilians, of course, will say how sorry they are but will not really understand. Two dogs I knew have died while I have been putting together this book. One was a Jack Russell called Button, who passed away peacefully in his sleep at boarding kennels while his owners were away; the other was a cheerful mongrel, one of the earliest friends Kudu made in the local park, who succumbed after an operation on her leg (she had been bitten by a brute during her afternoon walk). They came from very different backgrounds: Button's tycoon master buried him in a *grand cru* claret box in the pet cemetery in the grounds of his country pile, while the mongrel's owner – a freelance IT consultant in south London – retreated into his flat to mourn alone. But in their grief the two men were equals.

Dogs can make you healthier
29 May 2010

A dog-owning acquaintance was despatched to Battersea Park by his wife on a tummy-reducing mission – only to return home with a wifely secret unveiled. She had chivvied him with stories of health benefits from her walks with the family dog, so he took their terrier on his jog. When he opened the car door the dog sprinted to the park café and lay down, clearly expecting a prolonged coffee-and-gossip session.

I am ever more convinced that dogs are good for you. My sixteen-year-old stepdaughter is in the middle of her GCSEs; on revision days she insists – in a most un-teenage manner – on being woken for the morning Kudu walk, kick-starting body and brain for a day's hard slog with the textbooks. For good health we are all supposed to take at least 150 minutes of moderate exercise per week; Kudu would be delighted for me to hit the entire week's target in a pre-breakfast walk every day, and would cover double my distance without breaking his high-paced sniff-and-sprint.

Is there any hard evidence on the relationship between dogs and health? I asked a dog-owning GP, and was startled by the passion my question unleashed. So strongly does she feel that the health benefits of dog-ownership are under-estimated that she is considering a letter-writing campaign to the newspapers (under the *nom de plume* Dr Kay Nein) and she keeps her Spaniel in her surgery during consultations to push the point with her patients.

Lower cholesterol and blood-pressure, a reduced chance of your child suffering from asthma, better recovery prospects after a heart attack, lower stress levels and a stronger immune system: all this and more can be yours if you own a dog.

The Dogs Trust has ordered these benefits into a Canine Charter for Human Health, and the body of research they quote as supporting evidence is huge; if you follow the footnote trail you can only admire the inventiveness and dedication of some scientists. Imagine devoting your best years to a dissertation on 'Environmental influences on the expression of aggressive behaviour in the English Cocker Spaniel' (and who has ever heard of an aggressive Spaniel anyway?). And what can have inspired someone to investigate 'Animal companions and one year survival of patients after discharge from a coronary care unit'?

The most intriguing research concerned whether dogs can sniff out cancer. A letter to the medical journal the *Lancet* in 2001 reported the curious case of a Labrador called Parker. His master, a man in his sixties, developed a nasty patch of eczema on his left thigh, and Parker began to sniff at it obsessively. Eventually Parker's master took the hint and visited his doctor: analysis revealed that the lesion was in fact a basal cell carcinoma, and once it had been removed, Parker's interest in his master's left trouser-leg disappeared. (This story worried me a bit since Kudu has developed a habit of licking my legs after my bath, but since he does it to all of us, he may just like our soap.)

In 2004 a team of scientists in Buckinghamshire produced research to show that Parker was not a one-off. Over a period of seven months they trained six dogs to sniff for signs of bladder cancer in the urine of patients from their oncology department. At the end of the training period they were able to report that the dogs had managed a 41 per cent success rate in identifying urine from cancer patients, compared with the 14 per cent success rate that could have been expected by chance alone.

The scientists were very impressed by this but, based purely on Kudu's ferocious concentration when sniffing, I would have expected a better figure. As all owners know, dogs just love sniffing pee, and the scientists were offering this group 'freshly defrosted liquid specimens', which sounds like a doggy version of a fine Burgundy. I suspect the dogs were simply faking their failures in the hope of keeping the experiment going.

One piece of research I found in the footnote trail suggests that dogs increase self-esteem. This may be a claim too far. When my wife returns home after a day in her office, Kudu puts on a most melodramatic performance, squeaking quite shamelessly in ecstasy. When I get back after long hours in the BBC news factory, I have to be satisfied with a sceptically raised eyebrow and a heavy sigh – small reward for organizing my working day around Kudu's walking needs, and not at all good for the self-esteem.

Forgive me if this last paragraph is strong meat, but I am assuming only hardened dog-owners will have made it this far. Kudu is generally discreet about doing his morning business, favouring the trunks of trees and the leafy covering of bushes. But last weekend he unloaded his waste in the most spectacular and defiant fashion in the middle of a large group doing Military Fitness on Clapham Common; a rude message to modern faddishness, I feel sure, from all those generations of his ancestors who have kept their owners in good shape down the centuries.

*

When this column came out my dog-loving doctor friend telephoned me to say that she no longer keeps her dog in the consulting room. She had been forced to abandon the arrangement after an unfortunate incident during a cervical smear.

She had, as she delicately put it, just 'introduced the

speculum' when the dog, which had been snoozing quietly in its corner, had a rabbit-chasing dream and suddenly emitted a prolonged slobbery snuffle. 'Who have you got hiding in here?' shrieked the patient as she tried to jam her legs shut – tricky, since my doctor friend was, of course, standing between them at this stage. There was much laughter and no harm done, but since then the dog takes its naps elsewhere in the surgery.

7

Dog Love

DURING AN EMAIL exchange with a BBC colleague I enquired after the health of his Schnauzer, and received the following reply: 'Dog fine, thanks. She owes me £611 for dental maintenance and removal of a (benign) cyst. Nowadays I brush her teeth with a poultry-flavoured enzyme toothpaste. It has come to this. But I tell all my dog acquaintances to do the same or face large bills . . .'

The colleague in question is a contemporary; dog-owning definitely takes on a different character when you are middle-aged and your children have turned into young adults. We who have survived the soggy tests of nappy-changing and baby-feeding are more accepting of this kind of humiliation, and probably, though we do not admit it to ourselves, we miss the dependence of small children . . . and indulge our dogs to fill the void.

There is a revolting newly coined term to describe a dog that performs the role of child substitute: a 'furkid'. It is usually applied to the sort of miniature, shivering, over-bred and over-dressed toys that super-models and celebrities of the Paris Hilton variety carry about in their handbags – although for some of these types the line between dog as child-substitute and dog as fashion accessory has clearly become dangerously blurred.

One radio presenter – with a regular dog slot in her show – put out a press release to announce the Christmas list she was planning for her Bulldog:

- Handmade dog biscuits (£??)
- Tuffie Toys – strong enough to withstand a Bulldog's jaws (£60)
- Solid silver ID tag (£25)
- A designer collar from Holly & Lil (from £100)
- A luxurious new bed from Creature Clothes (£70)
- A selection of winter clothes including an Equafleece jumper, tweed coat from Holly & Lil and a hand-knitted pink sweater from New York (£200)
- A special festive afternoon tea at the very dog-friendly Milestone Hotel in London with her best friend the Miniature Bull Terrier (£50)
- One-on-one training sessions to teach her how to skateboard (£25 per session)

There is alleged to be some science to explain the development of the furkid phenomenon: apparently stroking a dog can provoke women to produce oxytocin, the same 'happy hormone' that is released by breast-feeding. Obviously this kind of frivolous tosh is a million miles from the sort of manly, unsentimental and outdoorsy relationship that my BBC colleague and I enjoy with our dogs, and I utterly repudiate any suggestion that Kudu is a furkid.

It is not just children who stir feelings of parental pride
12 June 2010

A neighbour who has recently joined the local dog-walking circle (with a very bouncy young Lab) has been commissioned to make a public sculpture of a Spaniel, and she approached me in the park to ask whether she could sketch some studies of Kudu as her model. This made me feel rather as I imagine Kate Moss's mum must have felt when she was told that her daughter would be on the cover of *Vogue* for the first time. I swelled with pride at the thought of the Dog's fine profile being immortalized in bronze.

Two days later I fell into an ambling conversation with a woman exercising her Jack Russell-Shih Tzu cross on Clapham Common. We spent a bit of time on the fun to be had in naming this surprisingly successful genetic experiment (a Jackshit?) and she then remarked — I am sure without malice — that Kudu's markings made him look like a cow. Shameful to confess, but I boiled with silent fury.

Quite why one should take pride in one's dog's looks I am not sure — it is not as if one can claim any genetic credit, as one can with children. But it is a widespread weakness.

The great Venetian painter Veronese suffered from it so badly that it got him into trouble with the Inquisition. In 1573 he was hauled up to account for certain 'oddities' in his vast painting *The Supper at the House of Levi*: he had slipped his dog into the centre of the canvas, where it gazes admiringly at a self-portrait the artist had also smuggled into the scene. Veronese explained that once he was satisfied that he had told his main narrative in a painting he liked to add 'figures according to my invention', if there was any room left, and he compared this to Michelangelo's use of nude figures in his religious paintings.

'In Michelangelo,' came the stern rebuke, 'thou dost not observe aught but the spiritual, and there are no drunkards, nor dogs, nor arms, nor any such buffooneries.' Leaving aside what this meant for Veronese (running foul of the Inquisition was a bad move, in those days), it seems rather rough on the dog to be bracketed with drunks and other 'buffooneries'.

I strive for honesty in evaluating Kudu's looks. He is a little short in the leg and, although certainly not flabby, a tad on the stout side. If he goes for too long without grooming the big brown marking along his back is bleached to what I am afraid is a gingerish tinge. But when properly looked after he is a mix of solid chocolate and milky white, and he is decorative around the house. I have acquired a few nice carpets in the course of my work in the Middle East, and he looks terrific stretched across the deep blues and reds of a Tabriz or a Hamadan rug.

Perhaps it was this happy doggy facility of harmonizing with gorgeous colours that inspired Veronese and several other Venetian painters to use so much dog imagery. The pictures of Veronese's contemporary Titian are absolutely stuffed with canine cameos.

Titian's dogs are usually portrayed in focused pursuit of their doggy interests, quite oblivious to the epic religious and mythical dramas unfolding on the canvas around them. In *The Last Supper* a dog gnaws contentedly at his bone under the table as an anguished Christ predicts his betrayal at the hands of Judas. In the *Bacchanal of the Andrians* there is a dog begging for titbits from a man at the back of the picture, not bothering even to glance at the wild orgy of binge-drinking and erotic indulgence in the foreground. In the wonderfully titled *Venus with*

Cupid, Dog and a Partridge, a small Spaniel with Kudu-ish colouring is trying to snaffle a bird off a window-ledge, unmoved to be sharing its couch with a disturbingly voluptuous nude with perfectly coiffed hair.

I have once or twice suspected Kudu of posing for effect, so I am reassured by Titian's idea that dogs go unselfconsciously about their business without worrying too much about the dramas of the humans around them. I am sure he is right, and if Kudu really were vain he surely would not show us his testicles quite so often.

Kudu memorably expressed his own aesthetic sensibility on a walk in Battersea Park. He ran ahead of me and dipped down out of sight, leaving the path to investigate the ducks on the lake. A passing jogger watched his progress and then pulled up, puffing, next to me. 'I don't know whether your dog is trying to make a point,' she said, 'but he has just crapped on the Barbara Hepworth.' I am rather fond of the huge, eye-shaped bronze sculpture that stands sentinel by the water's edge, but Kudu's gesture would find favour with a certain constituency of art lovers.

Before writing the column above, I researched the subject of dogs and art in the London Library. This venerable institution (it was founded by Thomas Carlyle) is in St James's Square, in the still handsome heart of London, and offers the sort of subtle pleasures that can only be enjoyed when you

have the time to linger over your task. All sorts of truly distinguished authors use it, so there is the thrill of wondering
which literary hero you might see at work (everyone dresses
with precisely the same degree of stylish dowdiness, mostly in
tweed, so the celebs can sometimes be difficult to spot). You
can search for your books among the stacks yourself, so there
is sometimes the excitement of serendipitously spotting something that perfectly fits your needs. And there is – at least I
suspect this – a discreet game of one-upmanship played
between the members with the titles they stack at their desks
in the Reading Room: the more obscure and erudite your pile
looks the better, and you can catch people glancing slyly at
their neighbours' choices while they try to work out the nature
of their research.

My pile usually contains titles like *The World's Greatest Dog
Stories* and *Dogs in Literature* – these may not be in quite the
same league as *Structure and Function of the Genitalia of Some
American Agelenid Spiders* or *Snorri Sturlson and the Edda; the
conversion of cultural capital in medieval Scandinavia* (both real
books, honestly) but the doggy theme does have 'em foxed, as
it were.

I puzzled for a while over whether to start my research
with Dogs or with Art – and was saved by one of those
moments of serendipity: I spotted, quite by chance, a book
called *Dogs in Painting* by William Secord. This took me
down an avenue of enquiry that had absolutely nothing to do
with the task in hand but proved intriguing none the
less: there is a very close relationship between the development

of dog portraits as a distinctive art form and the abuses that provoked the Bateson Report on breeding (see page 90).

Before the nineteenth century the concept of a breed was a relaxed one. The idea that particular kinds of dogs were suited to particular tasks has, of course, been around since the earliest days of dog-time – there is a famous seventeenth-century picture called *The Sleeping Sportsman*, which includes a sporting dog that is a dead ringer for Kudu – but there were no codes laying down what an ideal member of a breed should look like, and no one was much fussed about doggy family trees. And when dogs featured in pre-nineteenth-century British and European art they were generally adjuncts to the main event – providing extra colour or, in the Titian and Veronese manner, a dramatic device.

Queen Victoria changed all that. She was famously devoted to animals; she became patron of the Society for the Prevention of Cruelty to Animals as a princess in 1835 (giving the organization its 'R' prefix) and declared that 'No civilization is complete which does not include the dumb and defenceless of God's creatures within the sphere of charity and mercy.' She was especially fond of dogs and kept extensive kennels in Windsor Great Park, where she also maintained a small house from which she could watch her numerous dogs being brought out to play by the kennel man.

A photograph of one of the rooms in what became known as 'the Queen's Cottage' shows the walls completely covered with dog portraits. In 1836, just before Victoria's accession to the throne, the artist Edwin Landseer was commissioned to paint a portrait of Dash, her black-and-white King Charles Spaniel, for her eighteenth birthday, and it was the beginning of a lifelong passion for dog portraits.

Victoria's love of her dogs set the tone for the nation's canine culture, and her enthusiasm for having them painted effectively established a new art form. Britain was becoming richer, and dog-owning for pleasure became more widespread with the growth of a newly leisured class. With that came a snobby new interest in breed purity: it was suddenly fashionable to have a dog with a pedigree, and the Victorian writer Gordon Stables (a popular author of improving boys' adventure stories and, towards the end of his career, of a book called *The Dog: From Puppyhood to Age*) remarked in 1877 that 'Now nobody who is anybody can afford to be followed about with a mongrel dog.'

The first formal dog show took place in Newcastle in 1859. One of the judges was a certain Dr John Henry Walsh, the editor of the *Field* magazine, and a few years later he published his seminal work *The Dogs of the British Isles*, the first attempt to codify the ideal qualities of individual breeds. The Kennel Club was established in 1873 and produced its first official stud book a year later.

Charles Cruft was a key figure in the development of the Victorian canine culture. He began his dog career working as a clerk for James Spratt of Cincinnati, the first manufacturer of dog biscuits (when he opened a London branch, Spratt used Landseer pictures to promote his merchandise, and Victoria granted his company a royal warrant) but soon moved on to establish his eponymous shows. His breakthrough came when he persuaded Queen Victoria to show some of her pedigrees (her Collie and six Pomeranians, called Fluffy, Nino, Mino, Beppo, Gilda and Lulu). Unsurprisingly, given the deferential culture of the day, they all won prizes – and the modern tradition of the pedigree dog show was truly up and running. And, of course, those who won in Mr Cruft's shows wanted to have their dogs immortalized in dog portraits – just like the Queen's champions.

Victoria would, one feels sure, have been horrified by the way subsequent generations of breeders pursued prizes at the expense of canine health in the way Professor Bateson so shockingly described in his 2010 report (though I fear she might not have been entirely sound in the matter of furkids). She was a genuine dog-lover, and withdrew her own dogs from competition because there was an outbreak of distemper in her kennels shortly after the Crufts outing. But the evidence that the worship of breed purity was damaging dogs began to emerge very early. In 1911 the Hon. Mrs Neville Lytton wrote a book called *Toy Dogs and Their Ancestors Including the History and Management of Toy Spaniels, Pekingese, Japanese and Pomeranians* in which she reflected on the way modern breeding was distorting natural selection:

> Nature ruthlessly destroys the weaklings, the weeds, and the failures. The conditions of life are too uncompromising and they must die. The modern

man preserves them at infinite trouble and expense and offers prizes for them on the show bench. He breeds from individuals who would never naturally breed, which are too small, too feeble, or too deformed to propagate their species in a natural condition, and, moreover, often have a violent aversion in doing so. This is a grievous mistake.

Breeding must count for something: Mrs Lytton was the grand-daughter of that other great dog fancier, Lord Byron.

I am getting the silent treatment – and couldn't be happier
26 June 2010

While I am reporting from abroad I treasure the odd fix of Kudu-news when I phone home: there is something soothing about his trivial triumphs and disasters, especially when I am working somewhere rough. But it turns out he does not reciprocate the sentiment.

I have recently returned from ten days in Kyrgyzstan. One of my stories was being broadcast on the *Today* programme while my wife was driving to Clapham Common for the daily walk, and she loyally waited in the car with the radio on until the piece was finished. Kudu would have none of it: he gave the radio a head-butt and turned me off, demanding to be released for his run.

There is a famous story about the Russian actor Stanislavski, who used to keep his dog with him during rehearsals. It would sleep through the performance and only woke up when the actors were finished; Stanislavski claimed this showed the dog could tell when everyone had reverted to their 'real' personas. Evidently on the radio I am not real enough to detain Kudu from the urgent business that demands his attention whenever he sees a patch of green.

Though miffed by this doggy indifference, I could not help reflecting on how much Kudu would have enjoyed Kyrgyzstan. The twelve-hour drive from the capital, Bishkek, to Osh, the scene of the recent violence, is a quite spectacular journey up high mountain passes and through deep gorges. Roughly halfway there is a vast, open plateau, a bigger expanse of green than a dog could ever dream of.

This is where the country's nomads migrate in the summer to graze their herds, living in their traditional *yurts* amid the wild flowers, with snow-covered peaks gleaming in the distance. I saw several *yurt* dogs, standing sternly, like sentries, at the entrances to these circular tents. There were dogs herding goats, cows and even horses, and I watched one trotting happily at the heels of his master's mount as he rode high into rolling hills. What a doggy paradise. Even better, the usual human–animal relationship is reversed in these remote ranges: if a horse, a cow or a dog strays on to the road, the traffic gives way.

I spent several days in Osh just before the recent violence there erupted so dramatically, and was struck by the easy-going harmony between the city's human and canine populations (rather more harmonious than relations within the human population, as it now turns out). Most of Osh's dogs are feral, but they have developed good manners and are treated with respect in consequence. The balcony of my room looked down on a busy crossroads, and one evening I watched an elderly mongrel make its way purposefully across the street to the tree below me. It did its business discreetly under the branches – well away from the pavement – and then returned the way it had come.

A good book is essential on trips like this – there is always a certain amount of hanging around – and I took Andrew O'Hagan's jolly new novel *The Life and Opinions of Maf the Dog and His Friend Marilyn Monroe*, which is written entirely from the perspective of a Maltese Terrier, or Bichon Maltais (Maf is short for Mafia, the name being a little joke about the fact that he is a present to Marilyn Monroe from Frank Sinatra).

I didn't like Maf very much. He has picked up a quite staggering level of erudition from a puppyhood association with the writer and critic Cyril Connolly at his first home in Sussex, and tends to flash his learning around in a vulgar manner. There is a very funny scene in which he takes against Lillian Hellman and Edmund Wilson at a Manhattan book launch, and bites them both because of their offensive views (on Trotsky and the British respectively). But biting is not a nice thing for a dog to do, even if he shows good taste in his victims.

But Maf is an extremely effective narrative technique. Marilyn Monroe takes him everywhere – to parties, to her shrink, to her bed – so he is able to report everything, including her private moments. And O'Hagan plays very perceptively with the idea that dogs somehow intuit certain things about the people around them, absorbing moods and thoughts even when they are unspoken. Certainly one of the pleasures of Kudu's company is his capacity to give the impression that he knows what sort of spirits I am in, and is happy to lie around giving silent support if they are low.

Maff is a yappy little thing, and reading his *Life and Opinions* brought home to me how lucky we are to have a dog that does not bark. We know Kudu can bark – he does it in his sleep from time to time – but it is a form of communication he simply does not seem to favour. And here is an irony: the vuvuzelas, those droning bugles which drown out everything at World Cup matches, were, I am told, originally made from the horn of the kudu, the beast that gave our silent dog his name.

Dogs certainly change the dynamics of family relationships, but whether their influence on family life is entirely benign is a matter of some dispute. We made a quick checklist of pros and cons at supper one evening:

Pro-dog points

They stop arguments: it is absolutely impossible to raise your voice in front of most family dogs – they simply will not tolerate it. If you are really determined to have a domestic battle you have to do it in whispers.

They are a source of humour: Kudu has a gift for doing something silly with his ears at moments of tension.

They give you unconditional support after a hard day's work.

They keep the cats in order.

They never take issue with your views (unlike most other members of the family).

They provide a safe topic of conversation, which everyone can enjoy without worrying too much about delivering an unintentional slight or snub to someone else.

Anti-dog points

They are extremely strict about the importance of a hierarchical family structure; in our household this means I am the one to be feared, my wife is the one to be loved, and the younger generation are for playing with. Nothing can change this.

They ladder tights.

They provide an additional source of tension over the performance of domestic tasks – 'Has anyone fed/walked the dog?'

They put muddy paws on white bedspreads.

They are jealous, and will not tolerate any expression of affection between adults of even a remotely erotic nature. This is not a matter to dwell on in a book of this kind, but shut the bedroom door.

They also provide – as I discovered to my cost and recorded in the next column – an opportunity for devastating teenage commentary on the foibles of the older members of the household.

Dingoes are mere dunces compared with my Einstein
10 July 2010

Under the headline 'Your pet dog may be lovable . . . but it's none too bright', this newspaper recently reported the results of some research into the problem-solving abilities of domestic dogs and wild Australian dingoes (*Canis familiaris* and *Canis dingo*, to give them their proper scientific names).

Dr Bradley Smith, a psychologist at the University of South Australia, subjected a group of dingoes to what is known as the 'detour test'. This involves placing some food at the intersection point of a V-shaped transparent fence; the subject of the experiment is then shown the food from the wrong side of the fence, and has to work out how to get it. The dingoes very quickly (in twenty seconds on average) realized that they first had to walk away from the food in order to get back to it. Domestic dogs in the same situation apparently just sat there panting, looking puzzled, and appealed to their masters or mistresses for help.

The Australian papers ran the 'dogs are stupid' line even more strongly than the *Telegraph*: 'Dingoes deemed as top dogs, domestics dissed as dunces' was one headline. But problem-solving of this kind is a very narrow definition of intelligence; if you judged humans in the same way you would, for example, presumably rank the practical Crocodile Dundee above the scatty Wittgenstein.

The story prompted me to dig out the canine IQ test that has been languishing on a shelf since my stepdaughter, Rosy, gave it to me for Christmas. This does indeed test for a much wider range of abilities, and we decided to put Kudu through his paces.

His problem-solving skills are impressive: when we placed a treat under a mug in front of him he took a nano-second to work out that he could get the treat by knocking over the mug. He was good on language recognition (you say the word 'refrigerator' in the voice you usually use to call your dog, and if it responds, I am afraid it is not very clever) and not bad on short-term memory. He was weak in the social-learning section, and we did not quite have the energy for the experiment that involved moving all the furniture in a room to see whether he would notice. Overall I scored him at a creditable CIQ figure of 45: 'Your dog is in the high range of intelligence,' declared the booklet, 'and should be capable of doing virtually any task he is called upon to do.'

It is true that I did weight the scores a little to take account of environmental factors: I was cooking a barbecue while we did the tests, and Kudu was not unreasonably distracted by the smells at times. Rosy, who was acting as my research partner, took issue with my scoring and has refused to endorse the results. Indeed, she insisted on drawing up this disclaimer:

Contrary to what Edward may tell you, I'm sorry to announce, Kudu is not the glowing chosen one he is portrayed to be. I knew, whilst standing in front of the shelf debating whether or not to buy Edward a dog IQ test for Christmas, there would be a struggle. Not on Kudu's behalf, but on Ed's. You see, in my eyes, Edward is suffering from a form of denial in regards to our furry friend. A prime example of this was when we actually attempted the test. If Kudu did badly on a particular question, I was told to skip it out as the conditions were not up to the standard which they would be in a laboratory. However (shock horror!), if he did well, any concerns of this were lost and I was informed our clever little boy was too intelligent for these 'silly questions'.

Kudu has always been over-indulged and this was only one of many occasions that I have had to witness it. Not once have I heard Edward refer to anyone as 'sweetie', not even his children. Kudu, however, has been blessed with the name since setting foot in the household.

I'm sorry, Edward – you've been exposed!

A bit of a shock, that, from a sixteen-year-old! Rather than confront this unflattering picture of myself, I took refuge with Kudu in my writing-shed, where I am amassing a small library of great writers who have been dog-lovers. Here is the Greek historian Xenophon on his favourite bitch:

When we are at dinner she mouths one or other of us by the foot, as a hint that she should have her portion. She has more language than any other dog I ever knew, and can always tell you what she wants. Thus she was once whipped, when she had puppies, and to this day if anyone uses the word 'whip' she goes to the speaker, crouches down begging, and puts her mouth up to be kissed; then, jumping up with a grin, she puts her paws on his shoulders, and will not release him till all signs of threatening temper have vanished.

If Xenophon can be that sentimental, then, frankly, so can I!

An English tradition we can really live without
24 July 2010

Returning from the opera one balmy evening, my wife and I were tempted into the garden for a nightcap. The honeysuckle by the back door is exceptionally vigorous this year, and our jasmine has repaid the effort I put into a hard pruning: the scent is intoxicating. We sat in silence, drinking our wine, snatches of *Fidelio* chasing through our minds, and enjoyed the symphony of smells. It was just as an English summer night ought to be.

The nursery school next door is empty at night, so when we heard noises there we assumed it was foxes. Kudu told us otherwise, stock still and staring into the darkness (if it is foxes he does a wild circuit of the flowerbeds, inflicting maximum damage). There was a young man in the school garden – apparently playing with his dog.

He seemed reasonable when I remonstrated with him over the wall, but it pays to be prudent with an intruder in the dark, especially one accompanied by a large dog (Kudu had gone back to his nightly rounds of the shrubs by now). So I politely asked the man to leave and promised that I would not call the police unless he came back.

Just as we turned to the house his dog leapt at the branch of a tree, hanging on ferociously with its teeth. 'He'll be doing that to other dogs soon,' our intruder declared cheerfully. The primary-school garden was being used to train a fighting-dog. This realization provoked a not-at-all polite (and probably not entirely prudent) tirade from my wife about animal cruelty, and neither the dog nor its handler has been seen since.

The incident prompted me to do some research into dog-fighting, and I am afraid the tradition is every bit as English as the smell of honeysuckle on a summer's evening. The Romans were so impressed by the ferocity of English Mastiffs that they sent them to fight in the Colosseum. And little more than a mile from the scene of our nocturnal encounter, just over the Thames, there used to be a fearsome place called the Westminster Pit, which was entirely devoted to the pleasure of watching animals trying to kill one another.

In its heyday (the early nineteenth century), dog-fighting at the Pit was a highly formalized affair. The dogs – usually Staffordshire Bull Terriers – were weighed like boxers to ensure an equal contest. Some handlers smeared their dogs with pepper as a deterrent to biting, so each handler was allowed to lick the opponent's fur to check for cheating.

There was a line or 'scratch' drawn across the centre of the Pit, and the handlers would take their charges to opposing corners. Each round began with one of the dogs being allowed to attack first (known as 'scratching' or 'coming up to scratch'), and continue until one of the dogs 'faulted' by retreating from battle. The fight ended when a dog failed to 'come up to scratch' (thus presumably the modern use of the phrase) at the beginning of a round.

These battles could last for twenty rounds or

more, and even a death did not immediately end them. If a dog was killed the other dog had to 'stay at the corpse' for a further ten minutes. Then there was a break and a new round began. If it was the dead dog's turn to 'scratch', the fight was automatically lost. But if it was the live dog's turn and he did not 'come up to scratch' – through exhaustion or loss of spirit – he lost the fight even though he had killed his opponent.

These rules put a premium on aggression, and reading the way handlers boasted about what they euphemistically called the 'gameness' of their dogs is chilling. Dog-fighting was still legal in many American states until the 1960s, and British breeders used to export their dogs there. Here is one British enthusiast writing in the 1940s: 'It is natural that a sport demanding such gameness should produce some remarkable dogs. I saw a dog last year which refused to mate a bitch which was dead hot in season. Every time he was loosed he went straight for her throat and we had to choke him off eight times before he eventually mated her and he even tried to worry her when he was knotted.' For training a fighter, the same writer recommends an old tyre be 'hung up so he can jump up, catch hold and shake himself' – our young man had the right idea with the tree.

Most of us recoil at the idea of aggression. Kudu's

best friend, the Poodle Teddy, has been in trouble for dominating a Basset Hound while with his dog-walker, and it gave his mistress sleepless nights. She considered neutering him, but decided against it after canvassing opinion among the dog-walkers of Battersea Park (approaching total strangers about castration must, if you will forgive the pun, have taken balls). I am happy to report that Teddy has grown through his anti-Basset phase, and is as bouncy, cheerful and masculine as ever.

Fighting-dogs are a raw issue in the small park where I take Kudu for his afternoon walks – and it has sparked a turf war that is pure south London.

The park is in the middle of a very pretty conservation area of middle-class family homes, which is itself bordered by some of the roughest estates in the capital. Both the family-dog owners from the conservation area and the fighting-dog owners from the estates regard it as their preserve. There is no question about which side would win if it came to an open fight: some of the creatures you see being led in on studded leads make Cerberus look like a lapdog. But for the most part the two sides maintain an uneasy truce, with the fighting-dog owners monopolizing the dog run and the family-dog owners huddled defiantly together in the middle of the open grass, mobile phones at the ready to take pictures and call the police if anything untoward should occur. Kudu has narrowly escaped a couple of serious maulings – 'Honest, it's the first time he's ever done anything like that,' the owners declare, as they yank their slavering beasts back under control.

I find the idea of breeding and training a dog to fight profoundly repugnant, but I feel a little queasy about saying this because I do very much enjoy the way dogs are used in another sport that many people consider cruel. Occasionally I go shooting, and watching dogs work on a shoot is every bit as much fun as the sport itself. The discipline of good gun-dogs is awe-inspiring: despite quivering with excitement they will stay perfectly still during a drive until they are told to pick up a dead bird. But the real appeal of seeing them in action is the self-evident pleasure they take in doing something useful. I once met an engaging young black Cocker Spaniel out on his first shoot after being trained; every time he collected a dead pheasant he did a victory lap round his master's legs before dropping the bird.

Dogs can also be a great leveller on these occasions. At a partridge shoot (they are incredibly difficult birds to hit, and way above my level), I found myself next to a man I silently nicknamed 'the Wall of Death'. The sky above him was black with falling birds at every drive, while the lucky ones who chose my position were able to flutter unmolested to safety over my head. He had two beautiful Springers, and you could tell they were expensively trained by the way they sat patiently and attentively at his feet while the drive was in progress. As soon as the whistle signalled its end they were off about their picking-up duties, but one of them had an eccentricity: instead of bringing the birds back to its master, it simply arranged

8

A Dog's-Eye View

STUDIO LIFE IS seductive. You broadcast without stirring from a comfortable chair, and there is a small army of eager producers and skilled technicians on hand to support you. Some of the younger ones seem to admire you – unsettling at first, but you very quickly get used to the luxury. Taxis are booked to bring you in and take you home, and grumpy moods are tolerated. Best of all, no one can cut you off or meddle with your material: once the microphone goes live, the airtime is yours.

Reporting, by contrast, can be hard pounding, and is very much a young person's game. It means cramped planes and long flights, epic journeys in elderly and unsafe cars, endless, often grim, hotels; it means missing precious family moments and learning to love waking early and working late; it means long hours in the antechambers of those who think themselves mighty, and interviews doggedly pursued in the near-certain knowledge of disappointment.

The calling demands all sorts of indignities: I am writing this on assignment in Nigeria, and I have just spent half an hour in a down-at-heel Port Harcourt hotel hiding behind a curtain to re-create the right sound environment for a live broadcast. Worst of all, you lose control of your time because you live at the mercy of twin tyrants: deadlines and developments. And at the end of it all the fate of your material is decided by a programme editor back at base who may never have stirred beyond Shepherd's Bush.

And yet, and yet . . . it is hard to beat the thrill of being there when history is made, or seeing something that very few of your audience will ever see. I still get a charge out of the light-bulb moment, when the dynamics of a story click into place and you realize you have something worth telling your audience about. There is no drug quite like raw contact with real news.

My trip to see cancer-sniffing dogs in Buckinghamshire was not quite like interviewing Ronald Reagan in the Oval Office, or watching cruise missiles coming in over Baghdad, but it still had the wow factor every reporter hopes for when he or she sets out with notebook in hand.

Canines could be better value than quads and biopsies

7 August 2010

This newspaper recently reported the record price achieved by a sheepdog called Ron at Skipton Auction Mart: the fourteen-month-old Collie went for an astonishing 4,900 guineas (£5,145). 'In demonstrations on a hillside next to the auction mart,' the piece reported, 'Ron impressed the crowd by carefully rounding up one sheep which seemed determined to break away.' The *Telegraph*'s headline writer dubbed him 'the Rooney of the sheepdog transfer market'; his breeder, with a sheep farmer's canny calculations in mind, pointed out that buying a quad bike to do Ron's job would cost even more.

Kudu's record of crowd-pleasing performances is more varied. He recently played a blinder when a dog-curious family came to inspect him over Sunday lunch. The visit was sold to us by the father of the household on the basis that he and his wife were coming under pressure from Rachel, their eight-year-old daughter, to get a dog. It quickly became apparent that he was himself the main champion of the dog project (he is stepping down from a big job and will be at home more); Rachel was the one who needed convincing.

She had been biffed by a dog when younger and

reacted nervously to Kudu's rambunctiousness. But he quickly picked up on her mood, and when we suggested she might enjoy brushing him he was on his back almost before the brush was out of the cupboard. It was a hot day, and he was less enthusiastic about chasing his toys around the garden – whenever she threw one he tried to hide it under the table – but he played gamely through the afternoon, chased a tennis ball round the park for her and generally pitched his doggy charm so effectively that Rachel really was pushing for a dog by the time they left.

But two days later he let the side down badly on a photo-shoot in Richmond Park. The photographer Antoinette Eugster was trying to re-create a Wyeth painting of a young girl lying under a thunderous sky with a dog sitting in the background. My step-daughter Rosy cheerfully modelled the girl, and the sky was obligingly thunderous . . . but the dog just would not sit where he was told. So no hope of a modelling contract for Ron-style money!

I met a similarly camera-shy fellow at the Cancer Bio-detection Dogs charity in Buckinghamshire. I had been invited to a fund-raising event because I had mentioned the charity's research in an earlier column, and the organizers asked me, as the only journalist present, to take the obligatory photograph of smiling staff with one of those outsized cheques.

Jake, a black Lab in training as a sniffing dog, was required to be part of the group; I hope he is better at sniffing than he is at posing.

But the dog we saw in sniffing action – a Springer also, confusingly, called Jake – turned in a stunning performance. There was a contraption like a steel spider in the centre of the lab, and a urine sample was placed in a grip at the end of each leg. Jake's task was to identify which one came from a cancer patient – which he did every time and at great speed. His reward was a treat at the end of each round and tennis-ball fun with his handler at the end of the session.

Impressive, but could it ever be useful? Can we imagine cancer-sniffing centres staffed by Jake and his relations at NHS Trusts across the country? That, it seems, is not the point. Claire Guest, who runs the charity, explained they are using the dogs as researchers: if dogs can identify the smell associated with a cancer, she explained, humans can develop a mechanical system to detect it. That could mean a new screening system for, say, prostate cancer – the current test is notoriously unreliable and often involves an invasive and unnecessary biopsy. Whether this is good science I cannot say, but they are surely right that dogs know things we do not.

The demonstration by a companion dog for a diabetes patient was even more impressive – and his skills are more obviously useful. Rory, a Golden Retriever, sat in the middle of the lab at his handler's feet as she opened a jar with a sample from someone with a high blood-sugar level. He immediately put his feet on her shoulders and licked her face. When she failed to respond he padded across the room and collected a medical bag. The handler has type-one diabetes herself, and assured us this was no party trick: Rory frequently wakes her in the night when her levels are wrong.

It costs ten thousand pounds to get a dog to Rory's standard and settle him with a patient – but Claire Guest claims the NHS spends one million pounds per hour on diabetes-related cases. It is a bit like the quad-bike comparison from the breeder of 'Ron the Rooney of the sheepdog transfer market' at Skipton. And a dog is a lot more fun than a bike in the garage – or a doctor on call, come to that.

Seeing a really well-trained dog like Rory at work made me realize how remiss I have been about Kudu's training. He is certainly not yobbish – he has a naturally gentlemanly disposition – but his manners can be a bit rough on occasion, especially where hygiene is concerned. During one weekend away with him we were given a bedroom directly above the kitchen, and while changing for dinner we overheard our hosts discussing him in most unflattering terms (he had moaned about being locked in the boot room to dry off after a muddy walk). Dog etiquette is tricky territory; no two households have precisely the same set of dog rules, so taking your dog out socially is fraught with danger.

Dogs are conservative in their habits, and if they have been permitted to do something at home it is very difficult to persuade them that they should behave differently somewhere else; if, for example, you allow your dog to sleep on the sofa in your living room (we very much do not, I should add), he will certainly expect to do the same elsewhere, no matter how elegant, delicate and pale-coloured the sofa in question. And making judgements about when and where your dog will be welcome is complicated by the fact that the doggiest people often have the strictest rules. Most of our country friends assume that if they invite us to stay for a weekend the dog comes too – dogs are so much part of country life that we scarcely need to ask. On the other hand, many of them would never dream of letting a dog upstairs: country dogs tend to sleep locked up in the boot room, or even in kennels outside. Kudu – I blush to confess – sleeps in our bedroom.

I have tried quite hard to teach Kudu table manners so that he can join us in a pub after a walk, or on the terrace for lunch at the club where we play tennis. He still has not quite got over the idea that this constitutes being 'out', and being out is about having fun, so if I tie him to a table leg he will try to run off with the table. We did once try tying him to a bench next to the tennis court while we played, but watching a ball being hit about the place and not being able to run after it was simply too much of a torture.

Man's best friend can be a fiend, but I always defend him
21 August 2010

One of Kudu's friends returned from kennels several pounds lighter than at the start of his owners' summer break: exile so distressed him that he had gone on hunger strike. We are more indulgent. Kudu gets double-staffed while we are away – a dog-walker for the day and a house-sitter to keep him company at night.

She is a regular, and before we left for our two weeks in Turkey she came for an evening drink to remind herself of the house's plumbing eccentricities. Kudu had not seen her since last summer, but remembered her very well indeed: she got the usual frantic toy-offering ritual on her arrival, and once she was sitting he settled at her feet, muzzle on her knee and eyes fixed on her face in supplication.

For what? We allow him to sleep in our bedroom

and she does not. My guess is that he was getting his pleading in early.

I can trust him as a good host in his own home while we are away. I feel much more nervous when we take him somewhere as a guest. There was a searing Christmas moment at my brother's Hampshire house when he was young. The household rules included a 'no dogs upstairs' policy, which was being enforced with rigour because the house had just been decorated. After Midnight Mass, Kudu was shut in the scullery.

One of my sister's Spaniels was on heat, and although she spent the night in the car (the bitch, not my sister), Kudu had caught a whiff of those scrumptious smells. Whether it was lust or fear (of spending the night alone) I cannot say, but by stocking-opening time the newly painted scullery door was a wreck.

Readers will note I blame everyone but Kudu; dog-owners are much worse in this respect than indulgent parents. I know a good mother who was incapable of disciplining her over-exuberant Tibetan Terrier. When he memorably crapped in the middle of a food-laden cloth spread on the lawn of a grand country house for a *fête champêtre*, she airily declared that Tibetan Terriers are the reincarnated souls of Buddhist monks – as if this was a perfectly adequate explanation for the desecration of the *foie gras*.

Dog-indulgence was turned into a high art form

by a man called J. R. Ackerley, for many years the
literary editor of that now, sadly, defunct BBC institution the *Listener* magazine. I bought his book *My Dog
Tulip* as dog homework for the holiday, but found it
so funny I finished it before we left.

Tulip, an Alsatian, was, in the words of someone
who knew her, 'quite frankly . . . a terror'. Ackerley's
friends drop away as she fouls their carpets and
chases their cats, his social circle shrinking until his
only regular human contact is with the vet – though
he does enjoy a series of casual relationships with
other dog-owners, whose pets might provide Tulip
with sexual satisfaction. Ackerley is perplexed by his
social impoverishment, puzzled that his friends
seemed 'to resent being challenged whenever they
approached their own sitting or dining rooms'.

When Tulip upsets humans he always sides with
her. He decides that it is safer for her to defecate on
the pavement than in the road (the book was
published in 1965, before the idea of 'picking up'),
and sketches a wonderful scene on Putney
Embankment while she is about her business in the
mist of an early winter morning:

. . . a cyclist shot round the corner of the Star and
Garter Hotel towards us, pedalling rapidly . . . I don't
suppose I should have noticed this person at all if he
had not addressed me as he flew past:

178

'Try taking your dog off the sidewalk to mess!'

One should not lose one's temper, I know, but the remark stung me.

'What, to be run over by you? Try minding your own business!'

'I am an' all,' he bawled over his shoulder. 'What's the bleeding street for?'

'For turds like you!' I retorted.

The cyclist is, of course, completely right, but dog-owners will surely cheer for Ackerley.

Tulip is especially badly behaved at the vet, and she is rejected by several. My favourite vignette is the Spaniel that greets Ackerley at the third surgery he approaches:

He was standing quietly on a table with a thermometer sticking out of his bottom, like a cigarette. And this humiliating spectacle was rendered all the more crushing by the fact that there was no one else there. Absolutely motionless, and with an air of deep absorption, the dog was standing upon the table in an empty room with a thermometer in his bottom, almost as though he had put it there himself.

'Oh Tulip!' I groaned. 'If only you were like that!'

Yes, of course I have introduced that story in an Ackerley-ish way, because it reflects well on Spaniels.

The vet appointment for the annual booster is as much part of our summer ritual as sun-seeking, and Kudu behaved immaculately. He even insisted on coming back with the cats to cheer them up when they went for their jabs a week later.

Angling for acceptance where East meets West

4 September 2010

I have a wonder to report: I have seen a dog catch a fish.

It was early evening in the small Turkish port of Kaş. It had been a stinking hot day, and two shaggy German Shepherds were standing on the slipway into the harbour, enjoying the cool sea on their tummies. One suddenly executed an amazing bash-and-flip movement with his front paw, and a good-sized strip of flashing silver was ejected on to the quayside. The dog watched his prize until it stopped struggling. Whether it was destined for his bowl or his master's I do not know, because our own tummies rumbled and we were drawn to dinner.

Kudu suffered horribly during the London August heat. But that was as nothing to the high-summer furnace of south-east Turkey, and my heart went out to the dogs of Kaş. Most lay panting and immobile, piles of sweat-soaked fur on the pavements. The lucky few in shops cuddled their air-conditioning units as if they were radiators in winter.

Turkey famously mixes East and West. Its canine culture at first appears Middle Eastern: feral dogs roam the roads (I had two near misses in the hire car) and Western travellers who visited Istanbul in search of the exotic during the nineteenth century (like the French poets Lamartine and Nerval) remarked on the wild packs in the city's streets. Mark Twain wrote: 'I never saw such utterly wretched, starving, sad-visaged, broken-hearted looking curs in my life . . . I thought I was lazy, but I am a steam-engine compared to a Constantinople dog.'

Yet as the burning day cooled into evening in Kaş, a more English, even Home Counties doggy world was revealed. Well-dressed families with pedigrees on leads sauntered among the cafés around the mosque on the harbour front, and joggers with Labradors and Spaniels at their heels could be spotted sweating up the hill outside town.

It made me wonder whether Islam is as anti-dog as we assume.

There was a slew of press stories over the summer about dogs being turned off London buses because they might offend Muslims (no chance of Kudu suffering this indignity: he insists on being chauffeured and sits upright on the back seat in a plutocratic manner), and it was reported that even guide dogs had been treated in this way.

There is certainly a strand of scholarly Islamic opinion that regards dogs as ritually unclean. A dog-owning BBC colleague was astonished to find that a Muslim he had invited to lunch turned up with a spare suit: his guest said that he had been advised by his imam that the presence of even one dog-hair on his clothes would negate the power of his prayers.

But there is a dog story in the Koran that suggests the Prophet may have thought differently – and it is one of those intriguing texts that demonstrate how closely the great religions of Europe and the Middle East are related.

Its origins lie in a Christian legend. Around 250 AD, seven young noblemen in the ancient city of Ephesus – not so very far up the coast from our holiday port of Kaş – were accused of being Christians during the persecution by the Roman emperor Decius. Rather than deny their faith, they gave their money to the poor and retired to a cave in the mountains to pray. The emperor ruled that the mouth of the cave should be walled up, leaving them to die inside.

Three hundred years later – so the story goes – a local landowner broke down the wall so that he could use the cave as a cattle pen. The seven

Christian heroes were still alive – they had apparently slept through the intervening three centuries, and were startled to find themselves in a world where their faith had become mainstream. After a brief but joyful re-entry to the land of the living they expired, and were later made famous throughout Europe in early Christian writings.

Fast-forward three hundred years and we find the Prophet Muhammad being tested by the people of Mecca. The Jews of Medina have sent them a clever question: does Muhammad know about the Seven Sleepers? If he does, he is truly a prophet; if he does not, then he is a fraud. Muhammad duly produces Sura 18, The Cave, in which he tells the Seven Sleepers' story.

But Muhammad's version has a twist: he describes the Sleepers 'with their dog stretching out its forelegs' at the entrance to the cave, and the Sura is quite insistent about the dog's presence as a key element in the story. This dog, Katmir, is said to have stayed awake for the full three centuries, watching over his charges, and some sources suggest it is one of the nine animals that will be allowed into Paradise. Ritually unclean? Surely not.

Kudu is certainly unclean in a more literal sense. Returning from baking Turkey to find London awash with rain delighted me for a while, but I very quickly tired of damp walks. Kudu, however, is absolutely

jubilant that the dog-days of summer are over, and
takes full advantage of every puddle available.

A month or so after writing the column above I was recording
a Radio 4 programme in Istanbul, and managed to escape duty
for a couple of hours to wander round the Grand Bazaar. I
found a stall selling nineteenth-century illuminated pages from
Ottoman story books; they were the most beautiful artefacts,
but very expensive, and I was having terrible trouble deciding
which one to buy until an illustration of the Seven Sleepers
story emerged from the pile. The artist had painted Katmir in
a style similar to that of a *Snoopy* cartoon, and he has a definite
paunch in the picture. What is more he is, unlike the Katmir
of the Koran, clearly asleep, which suggests an Ottoman play-
fulness in the treatment of the sacred texts. It was an irresistible
buy.

The news that Kudu's column in the *Telegraph* was being
put to sleep reached me on return from our summer holiday in
Turkey. Whenever I lose a contract or have a show canned it
seems to happen in the most awkward and unlikely
circumstances.

Many years ago I had a weekly radio programme, which
was axed as part of a network shake-up. There were lots of
stories in the papers confidently predicting its demise, so when
the executive in charge asked me up to her office after the
show one morning, I had a pretty good idea of what to expect.
Gloriously, the lift got stuck, and since it was full of people, we
could not very well have the conversation we both knew was

coming. We made painful small talk for the half-hour or so that it took for the engineers to do their thing.

By the time we were finally deposited back on the ground floor I was running late for my next appointment, and politely explained that I would have to go. Could we perhaps meet another time? I made the enquiry sound as innocent as I could, but I was fairly sure she would have left this unpleasant task until the last possible moment, and would be in agony over what to do. It was some small satisfaction to force her into delivering the bad news outside on the pavement, with my taxi's engine idling nearby.

The call to come into the office to be told I had lost my role as the presenter of the *One O'Clock News* came while I was Christmas shopping in Harrods, and the bad news about the *Today* programme reached me in the car park of a hotel in Harrogate, where I had just addressed a literary lunch. Neither of those was funny at the time.

The first hint that the Kudu column was for the chop came when my BlackBerry started pinging with emails at the baggage carousel at Gatwick; one of them was ominously titled 'CHANGES'. By the time I had got through to the relevant editor I was on the Gatwick Express, so the phone kept cutting out. But I got the message in the end. My broadcasting work had picked up again by then, and when I hung up I reflected that Kudu had, in a characteristically unfussy doggy way, Done his Duty by seeing me through a troubled time, and could retire from literary life with his head held high.

Much to be learnt from taking a dog's-eye view of things

18 September 2010

In one of the earliest of these columns I introduced Bertie, a wise Border Collie with a remarkable command of the English language. His owner, a distinguished QC, claimed that Bertie could always understand the word 'ride'. However it was used ('Let's go for a ride' or 'Let's go riding') and whatever the tone (a shout or a whisper), Bertie would always trot off to the tack room for the treat of a horse-led ramble through the Hertfordshire countryside.

Time has rolled on, and Bertie has passed a milestone. One sad day this summer his master (a judge now, so older and wiser himself) invited Bertie out for their usual post-Sunday lunch expedition. Bertie shook his head and retreated to his basket. 'Dogs know,' said my friend the lawyer, 'when it is time to call it a day.'

So does this column. Kudu is retiring from public life, and this will be the last of his regular rambles in the pages of the Saturday *Telegraph*.

His celebrity has been entirely accidental; these columns were never planned. When I lost my slot on the *Today* programme, the *Telegraph* was kind enough to offer me a home here. Had anyone said to me, when I began in journalism more than three decades ago, that I would wind up writing about walking the dog, I should have laughed. But the experience has been unexpectedly rewarding.

As a civilian dog-walker I always suspected that the dog's-eye view of the world had something unusual to offer. But it was only when I began writing about Kudu's life that I realized quite how rich the canine perspective can be. There is no field of human endeavour – not art nor politics, not science nor society – which does not yield something new when approached in this way.

Some animal behaviourists recommend that if you really want to understand your dog you should spend an afternoon on your hands and knees, watching the world at skirt level and relishing the proximity of smelly feet and decaying odds and ends that have escaped the broom. Spiritually speaking, that is where I have been for the last sixteen months.

Lobby correspondents are sought out by cabinet ministers with secrets to spill and leaks to spring; in the same way a dog columnist is a magnet for those with good doggy stories to tell. Only this week I picked up a cracking indiscretion doing the rounds in Whitehall: some years ago one of my grander BBC colleagues found himself next to Prince Edward at a social occasion. Searching frantically for something to fill a conversational vacuum, he alighted on the fact that both he and the prince had recently become fathers for the first time. 'A bit of a shock, this children business,' he remarked. 'Not to us,' came the royal riposte. 'We had dogs.'

Kudu has taught me something important about journalism. Keats famously defined Shakespeare's genius as 'Negative Capability, that is, when a man is capable of being in uncertainties, mysteries, doubts, without any irritable reaching after fact and reason'. Most of my journalistic career has been, precisely, an 'irritable reaching after fact and reason'. From Kudu I have learnt the value of the imaginative meander – sniffing about where the fancy strikes and (if you will forgive the pun) following a lead, without worrying too much about where it will take me. Kudu stories have a beginning and a middle, but often no particular end.

Earlier this summer this newspaper (among others) reported research that suggested dogs learn to behave like their owners. Since Kudu is generally regarded as a well-mannered and affectionate creature, I remarked to my wife that this reflected well on us. 'He behaves like you,' she said, 'only in that he insists on having his back scratched and snores heavily at night.'

I like to think that he has also picked up an interest in literary work, so the final word goes to him.

*

You cannot imagine what a strain it has been these
past months, providing material for my Master's
writing. I know his deadlines, and sometimes I
wake up sick with worry.

The celebrity fishbowl is a terrible place to live. I
like sitting comfortably upright on the back seat of
the car – if I press my nose against the window I
can spot the park coming up. But why does that
mean I must be described as a 'plutocratic' poseur,
as I was in the most recent column? Of course I pull
on the lead, eat sticks and defecate in embarrassing
places – that is what any self-respecting Spaniel
does.

What a relief to stop worrying about the literary
weight of everything I do. When I sniff a bitch's
bottom I shall no longer wonder whether it might
inspire some metaphor or flight of fancy: it will be
just what it is – a bitch's bottom. I can again enjoy
the thingness of things.

Yours
Kudu

The *Telegraph* subs, who, by and large, had been kind to my
copy, made two surprising changes to this final flourish. 'Bitch's
bottom' became 'the backside of a passing Schnauzer', which is
not at all the same and suggested a regrettable and un-
characteristic outbreak of prissiness or Political Correctness in

the *Torygraph* newsroom. It annoyingly frustrated my childish ambition to slip a rude phrase into a respectable national broadsheet.

And the reference to Kudu enjoying 'the thingness of things' became, intriguingly, 'I can once again dwell in the thingliness of things, as Heidegger said'.

Clearly, I thought, the work of a philosophy graduate who feels his academic training is undervalued on the subs desk. Heidegger was a Nazi, and the British philosopher Roger Scruton memorably observed that his most important work, *Being and Time*, 'is formidably difficult − unless it is utter nonsense, in which case it is laughably easy. I am not sure how to judge it, and have read no commentator who begins to make sense of it.' But Heidegger is clearly fascinated by such ideas as the 'jugness of a jug', and he wrote extensively on Immanuel Kant and his concept of 'things-in-themselves', or *noumena*.

The term is variously defined as 'objects as they are in themselves independent of the mind' or − in a strictly Kantian sense − 'the things that underlie our experience' but *'are not themselves objects of possible experience'* (my italics). That is roughly what I was driving at (at least I think it is). I do not believe that I have the capacity to grasp the essential bitch's bottomness of a bitch's bottom, but Kudu, I suspect, does. His experience of the world is more direct, less filtered by the intellect. Kudu knows *noumena* in a way we humans never can.

Dogs are aids to philosophy in the simple sense that their constant demands for walks force one to spend time in a way that is conducive to solitary thought, and in the more subtle sense that regular interaction with another Being encourages one to reflect on the nature of one's own Being. But they are also what you might call anti-philosophers: they have the capacity to exhibit abstract qualities (affection, concern, loyalty and so on) in an entirely instinctive way, without any of the reflection or agonizing that humans like to engage in when we try to decide how we should act.

Kudu's contribution to the History of Thought brings to mind Dr Johnson's famous rebuke to Bishop Berkeley, the father of idealism, or immaterialism, who suggested that things only exist in so far as we perceive them – so that the answer to the conundrum 'If a tree falls in the forest, and no one hears it, does it make a sound?' must be no. Johnson's response to this is recorded in Boswell's *Life*: 'After we came out of the church, we stood talking for some time together of Bishop Berkeley's ingenious sophistry to prove the non-existence of matter, and that every thing in the universe is merely ideal. I observed, that though we are satisfied his doctrine is not true, it is impossible to refute it. I never shall forget the alacrity with which Johnson answered, striking his foot with mighty force against a large stone, till he rebounded from it – "I refute it *thus*." '

In similar fashion Kudu offers a refutation of Socrates, who declared that 'The unexamined life is not worth living.' Kudu lives just such a life (the fact that it is endlessly examined by me does not count) but it is self-evidently – resplendently, indeed – worth living.

Cruel Crossing
Escaping Hitler Across The Pyrenees
Edward Stourton

The mountain paths were as treacherous as they were steep – the more so in the dark and in winter. Even for the fit the journey is a formidable challenge – many of those who made the attempt during the Second World War were malnourished after weeks on the run and had been cooped up hiding in barns and attics. Many never even reached the Spanish border.

Today, the bravery and endurance of thousands of people who climbed through the Pyrenees to escape the Nazis are remembered each July with a walk from St-Girons in France to Esterri d'Aneu in Spain. Embarking on the *Chemin de la Liberté* – the toughest and most dangerous of wartime routes – Edward Stourton finds his fellow pilgrims each have personal reasons for commemorating the escape lines. Family histories include midnight scrambles across rooftops and drops from speeding trains, burning Lancasters, bayonets jabbed into haystacks, doomed love affairs, horrific murder and astonishing heroism. The lives of the men, women and children who were drawn by the war to the Pyrenees often read as breathtakingly exciting adventures, but they were led against a background of intense fear, mounting persecution and horrific risk.

Drawing on interviews with the few remaining survivors and the families of those who were there, Edward Stourton's vivid history of this little known aspect of the Second World War is shocking, dramatic and intensely moving.

Coming soon from Doubleday